Pers Mgmt.

CW01067017

FIT FOR WORK

FIT FOR WORK

A Practical Guide to Good Health
for People Who Sit on the Job

Scott W Donkin

**KOGAN
PAGE**

First published in the United States of America in
1987, entitled *Sitting on the Job*, by Houghton Mifflin Company,
2 Park Street, Boston, Massachusetts 02108.

This edition first published in Great Britain in
1990 by Kogan Page Ltd, 120 Pentonville Road,
London N1 9JN.

British Library Cataloguing in Publication Data
A CIP record for this book is available from
the British Library.

ISBN 0-7494-0350-0
ISBN 0-7494-0264-4 Pbk

Typeset by DP Photosetting, Aylesbury, Bucks
Printed and bound in Great Britain by
Biddles Ltd, Guildford.

To my wife, Mary Pat, whose constant support and incredible patience transformed these thoughts and ideas into reality. She taught me, by example, that life and work should be fun and that others need to be given the opportunity to realise this concept.

Acknowledgements

This book, throughout its creation, has been a team effort even though some participants didn't know they were members of the team. Especial thanks are due to:

Joseph J Sweere (contibuting editor), Jan Kelley Weinberg (illustration and design), John and Elizabeth Laugen, Thomas M Wolff, Rani Karen Lueder, Mark Hirschfeld, Tom Cebuhar and Sue Bernt, Jan Beckwith, Jolene Anderson, the doctors and staff of the Rohrs Chiropractic Center, Sandra Wendel, Larry Pelter, Kerry Jones and Tom Chapman, Charlene Henninger, Madelein Mathis, Larry McPhillips, Marvin Schlegel, John Sullivan, Lorrie Vojtech and Sandy and Dean Weinmeister.

One look at the bibliography in the back of this book will tell you that there are many more contributors. These doctors, scientists and researchers used their talents to fulfil their desire to help their fellow humans discover meaningful information. Many of their facts, concepts and ideas have been integrated into this book. They certainly deserve a great deal of credit for the guidance this book provides to help its readers become happier, healthier, and more productive in their chosen occupations, and enhance the quality of their lives.

The information and content of this book are not intended to cure all the problems which occur in environments and occupations which require sitting. Nor does it purport to cure all sedentary workers' physical and stress-related problems. It is intended to provide a framework of understanding about these occupations, so that individuals and companies or businesses can discover how to improve or enhance conditions which would be beneficial to everyone concerned. If you suffer from any physical or stress-related disorders or conditions, present or past, seek professional guidance before attempting any changes. Consult with management or your supervisors before instituting work area or work environment changes.

Contents

Acknowledgements   5

Preface   9

Introduction   13

1. **Your Body**   15
   Basic body mechanics 17; Habits and time 22; The
   advantages of sitting properly 24

2. **Your Work Space**   27
   Your own work area 27; Your chair 28; Your work
   surface 31; Arrangement of work materials 38;
   Computerised work areas 39; Non-computerised work
   areas 41; The visual display unit 44

3. **Your Office Environment**   46
   General lighting considerations 46; Computer terminal
   lighting 47; Room temperature and draughts 48; Noise
   51

4. **Common Physical Complaints**   53
   How injuries occur 53; Caution 55; Other causes of
   physical symptoms 55; Eye strain 56; Back pain 60;
   Neck pain 63; Shoulder and arm symptoms 64; Wrist,
   hand and finger symptoms 66; Leg and foot symptoms
   69; Headaches 72; Fatigue 75

5. **Stress** 78
Understanding stress 78; Progressive relaxation 82;
Deep breathing 83; Positive imagery 84; Focusing 85;
Helpful relaxing practices 86; Exercise 86; The stress-
resistant person 88

6. **Exercise** 91
Requirements of exercise 94; Personal body inventory
95; Special hazards of sitting 99; Exercising during the
working day 101; Micro-breaks 102; Mini-breaks 104;
Macro-breaks 105; Lunch breaks 105; Special exercises
106

7. **Sleep** 110
Principles of sleep 110; Proper sleeping positions 115;
Caution 121

8. **Replacing Undesirable Habits** 122

The Choice is Yours! 127

Appendix
1. Personal Lifestyle Inventory *128*
2. Nutrition *131*
3. The Orthopaedic or Kneeling Chair *133*

Bibliography 135

To the Reader 136

Preface

Millions of people who earn their living while doing sedentary work needlessly endure excessive pain, stress and strain during their work and in their lives. Many people feel that pain, stress and strain are necessary evils in today's civilised, sophisticated and technological society. I believe that, although these complaints are common, they are not normal. The physical and emotional effects of pain, strain and negative stress represent signals or cries for help. First, we must admit that these problems exist. Then we can discover and implement positive solutions.

While in pursuit of improving the quality of service to my patients and community, I enrolled in post-graduate courses offered by the International Academy of Chiropractic Industrial Consultants (IACIC) – a group of concerned professionals who are making great strides in assisting manufacturing industries while making their workplaces safer, in educating workers to prevent injuries and promote good health and well-being, and in helping to place workers in jobs for which they could be most valuable. The benefits to these manufacturing industries have been phenomenal. Fewer workers have been injured on the job. Those who were injured usually recovered faster. Workers' compensation insurance premiums paid by the employers have been reduced.

Everyone involved in the programme is benefiting. Workers have a safer place in which to perform their tasks. They are realising what they can do to enhance their health and productivity, and that their employers care about them and are interested in their well-being. Employers are seeing happier, healthier, more productive workers who are less likely to leave their jobs for a better place to work. As a result, costs for training new workers have been greatly reduced. Since worker related expenses have been reduced and productivity has increased, employers are finding themselves more competitive in the market-place.

After witnessing the positive effects of the programme in manufacturing industries, it occurred to me that other industries could also benefit from these concepts, especially those which employ sedentary workers. In my chiropractic practice, I began to observe that people who earn their living while sitting seem to recover from certain physical conditions and injuries at a slower rate and with greater difficulty than others.

One particular case comes to mind. One of my patients suffered a severe neck and back injury as a result of a road accident. I had been treating her for quite some time for the effects of this injury. She had gained relief from many of her original complaints, but she still suffered severe headaches at times. The treatment would alleviate the headaches but then they would recur. A pattern began to emerge: she had fewer symptoms during weekends and holidays. We finally discovered that at work she frequently looked through the lower lens of her bifocal glasses in order to inspect information which appeared on a visual display unit. The viewing screen was positioned too high for her and she had to tilt her head backwards repeatedly to see the screen, thus aggravating her injured neck, and contributing to her recurring headaches. Once the appropriate changes were made to the height of the screen, she recovered and was discharged from treatment for the effects of this injury. I discovered that similar situations were common.

A system was evidently needed to discover how an individual feels about his or her workplace and to determine whether conditions in the work area or work environment (or in the individual) interfere with the worker's ability to perform his or her tasks efficiently, consistently and accurately, and to do so without pain, discomfort and stress.

One of the primary solutions is to help people understand the nature of their work and work environment so they can learn how to achieve greater comfort and productivity in their work areas and how to counteract the possible negative effects of the type of work they perform.

This book was written with this goal in mind. It is fully illustrated, as illustrations will enable you to capture and understand important concepts more easily.

It would be impossible to describe and explain every situation in everyone's unique work setting. The content, design and format of this book are intended to provide concepts which will help you to understand what changes should be made to your work area and habits, and why these changes are essential for you and your work.

A well-designed chair cannot achieve its maximum effect unless you, the user, understand how to make it fit your body and use it in the manner for which it was intended. The same is true for well-designed work areas, equipment and the other tools you use to perform your tasks. They can't help you unless you understand their proper function and use them appropriately.

This book describes practical methods designed to help you create a better 'fit' between your work environment, work area and your body. It also contains practical techniques to reduce stress, counteract the effects of long periods of sitting, and thus enhance the quality of your life.

Introduction

This is an exciting day for you because you have discovered information that will help you not only to survive, but thrive in your chosen occupation. This book will outline and explain information about you and your body as well as fundamentals of your surroundings at work. You will learn how work can affect your body and how to reduce or eliminate problems affecting your health, well-being, job performance and job satisfaction.

You will learn how stress affects you and practical techniques to turn its negative effects into positive action. You will also learn how essential it is to fit your body properly into your work area as well as to change your work area to fit your body.

This book will provide you with a great deal of knowledge about you and your work and offer a number of solutions: you will be encouraged to take steps which will benefit you and to keep to these recommendations in order to achieve maximum results. Knowledge, action, enthusiasm and consistency are the keys you need to unlock the doors to a healthier, happier and more productive future in your chosen occupation.

Your work environment may seem like a man-made jungle that is as menacing and stressful as a natural jungle. One can survive and thrive in a natural jungle, if its rules or laws are understood and obeyed. If these rules are ignored, one is sure to perish. Less life-threatening, but every bit as important to you, is knowing and understanding the laws which govern the physical and mental demands of your work. Your ability to survive and thrive in your chosen occupation is directly dependent on your knowledge and understanding of these laws and your ability to make them work to your advantage.

Many employers will be pleased to learn that you are participating in a positive growth experience; knowledgeable employers understand that whatever you do to help make yourself more comfortable and healthier will also help you to become more enthusiastic, productive and a greater asset to the company or business.

First, you must know and understand your body and how it functions. With this knowledge you will realise the value of the changes you can make to combat effectively the areas that may be causing you problems in your work activities. You really have nothing to lose and much to gain, so let's begin our journey to find the knowledge that will allow you to make changes you probably didn't think possible.

1
Your Body

Your body is a miracle of engineering, physics, chemistry and electronics – all these combine to form what man has not been able to duplicate and probably never will.

The core of your physical body is the nervous system. The brain, spinal cord and peripheral nerves regulate all the functions of your body. Virtually every cell in your body has a nerve supply that communicates information to and from your brain. In fact, it has been said that if you took everything away from the body except the nerves, the remaining nerve network would create an exact replica of the human being. You would even be able to recognise the individual! When your parents were children, it was believed that once the heart stopped the individual was no longer alive. Modern science now recognises that physical life ends when the brain dies. The brain is the source of all the energy that travels through the nervous system and human life is not possible without this nerve energy (Figure 1.1).

Nerves are very delicate and sensitive, so protection is provided in the form of calcium-laden bones. The skull protects the brain and the spinal vertebrae protect the spinal cord (Figure 1.2). A layer of protein liquid (cerebro-spinal fluid) surrounds the brain and spinal cord to provide nutrition and act as an effective shock absorber. There is little movement between the bones of the skull, but the neck and back must be flexible to allow smooth and graceful motion, and a series of bones called vertebrae allow this motion while still giving protection. The vertebrae are stacked on top of each other like building blocks and are separated by doughnut-shaped cushions

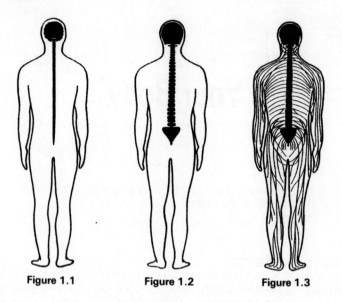

Figure 1.1   Figure 1.2   Figure 1.3

Figure 1.1   *The brain and spinal cord control and regulate the human body*

Figure 1.2   *The brain is protected by the skull and the spinal cord is protected by vertebrae forming the spine*

Figure 1.3   *Spinal nerves leave the spinal cord through openings between the vertebrae to serve all parts of the body*

called discs. The discs hold portions of the vertebrae together and provide shock absorption for the body in standing and sitting postures.

Spinal nerves leave the spinal cord through openings between the vertebrae in order to serve all the parts of the body (Figure 1.3). The spinal bones must be anchored together but still allow motion, so the body has strong, but elastic ligaments (Figure 1.4). These ligaments help to hold the bones together while the muscles, by their ability to contract and relax, actually move the bones. This is true not only for the vertebrae, but also for the bones and joints of the arms, hands, legs and feet. Many muscles narrow into tendons which are attached to the bones for extra leverage. The bones provide the levers; the ligaments hold the bones together; and the muscles move the bones. All this action is controlled by the nervous system.

Figure 1.4 *The spine is made up of vertebrae and discs that are held together by ligaments and muscles*

Basic body mechanics

Your body must be able to move from one place to another, so your legs have joints and powerful muscles (Figure 1.5). The feet and legs provide the foundation for your body. The legs are attached through the hip sockets to the pelvis which, with the sacral bone, provides the foundation or base for the spine and the rest of the body.

The physical body could be viewed as a vehicle or machine and must obey the universal laws of physics and engineering. This is

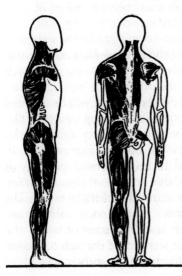

Figure 1.5 *Muscles, through contraction and relaxation, allow us to move and help us to maintain balance and posture*

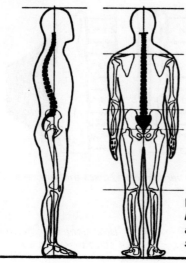

Figure 1.6 *Ideally, the spine should be vertical when viewed from behind and S-shaped when viewed from the side*

where balance becomes important. The laws of gravity reign over all physical structures and this includes the human body. Your upper body must be balanced over your legs, otherwise you would tend to fall over. Ideally, your spine should be straight up and down (vertical or plumb) with your shoulders equally balanced over your body (Figure 1.6). This isn't always the case, and it is this quality of uniqueness about your body that you must become aware of.

Most of us deviate to some extent from perfectly normal balance, but the extent to which you vary from normal can be the extent to which you experience physical stress and strain which can eventually become aches and pains. For example, if you have a fallen arch in one foot, or one leg shorter than the other, your hips and pelvis will become distorted and your total body balance will be affected (Figure 1.7). When the nervous system is working properly, the body has a marvellous ability to take account of any imbalance by twisting and turning other parts of the body to compensate. If, however, vertebrae become lodged in an abnormal position or restricted in their movement during this process of compensation, or as a result of trauma or stress, nerve interference can result. The term commonly used to describe this dysfunction is subluxation. Subluxation is the abnormal position and/or motion of bones at a joint that is less than dislocation, but significant enough to crowd, stretch or otherwise interfere with the function of the nerve fibres

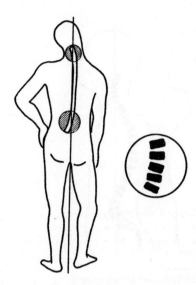

Figure 1.7 *Deviations from normal body balance can cause physical stress and strain*

which, in this case, exit between the vertebrae (Figure 1.8). This becomes a source of spinal weakness, instability, muscle spasm and nerve interference, which produce such symptoms as pain, burning, numbness and tingling.

Here is where another law of nature comes into play: a structure that bears more stress and strain tends to wear out faster. This is similar to the uneven wear you see on your car tyres if the wheels are unbalanced or out of alignment. These same forces or laws of nature affect you and your body. The objective here is to make you aware that these laws exist and show you how they can affect you.

Viewed from the side, the spine should normally have four curves: a backward curve at the base of the spine, a forward curve at

 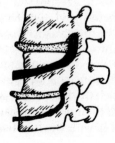

Figure 1.8 *Vertebrae that are not properly aligned or that do not move normally can cause strain, nerve irritation and abnormal wear of joints over time*

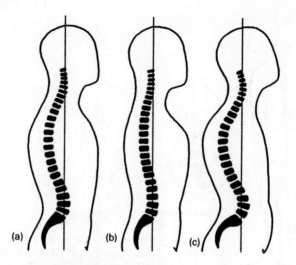

Figure 1.9 *(a) Normal spinal curves (b) Reduced spinal curves (c) Increased spinal curves*

the lower spine, a backward curve at the upper spine, and a forward curve at the neck. The two forward curves should counterbalance the two backward curves to allow the entire trunk to remain balanced over the centre of gravity (Figure 1.9). This S-shaped configuration is designed to provide a means of shock absorption in much the same way as a coiled spring absorbs shock. These forward and backward curves are normal and desirable in both the standing and sitting positions. If the spinal curves are reduced, producing a 'ramrod' alignment; or are bowed too much, producing a 'swayback' or 'hunchback', biomechanical stress and strain are created. You should, therefore, work to preserve these normal curves in both the standing and sitting positions.

It would be easier to sit in a conventional chair if our bodies were square, box-like and all the same size, but that just isn't the case. We are designed with curves, bends, and in different sizes and shapes. Our contours do not fit well into a straight chair. As the saying goes, 'You can't fit a square peg into a round hole.' Ideally, a chair should fit and support the unique shape and contour of the body (Figure 1.10). The extent to which a chair does not provide this fit and support is the extent to which the body experiences physical strain.

It would be to your benefit to adjust or modify your chair to fit you as much as possible. If you have a straight-backed chair, you may

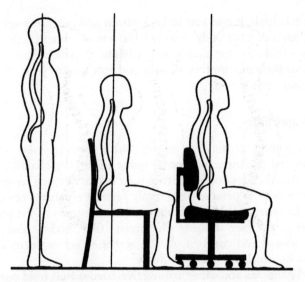

Figure 1.10 *The human body is best supported by a chair that fits its unique size and shape*

need to fit a specially designed supportive pillow in the space between the chair and the natural forward curve of your lower back (Figure 1.11). If you have a well-designed contoured chair, you need to make sure it fits your spinal curves properly. If the backrest is too

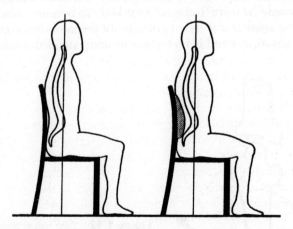

Figure 1.11 *A specially designed pillow will help to make a straight-backed chair fit the lower back*

low or too high, it can add to back strain and put pressure on the wrong parts of your body. You will learn more about proper sitting positions from the explanations in Chapter 2, which illustrate how to fit your body into your work area and how to alter your work area to fit your unique body.

Habits and time

At this point you may be asking, 'Why should I take action to improve my posture and consistently adjust my chair to fit my body?' Another law of human nature is that we are creatures of habit and as time passes, we actually become creatures of our own habits. In other words, our bodies tend to conform to the positions and postures they assume the most. Our bodies also try to accommodate and conform to the activities we perform and the manner in which we perform them.

The ligaments and other connective tissues that hold our bones together have what is referred to in engineering terms as both 'elastic' and 'plastic' properties. The elastic property of these tissues allows them to spring back to their original form when a stretch or movement is completed. The plastic property gives them a putty-like character and they tend to remain at a tension or in a position that they are most familiar with. If you spend the majority of your working day slumped at your desk with your head flexed forward or you are always turning in one direction, the connective tissues will eventually allow the body to conform to those abnormal positions. Unknowingly, you are 'training' your body to become unbalanced.

There is another important point about the joints and connective tissues to bear in mind before you can understand the solution to

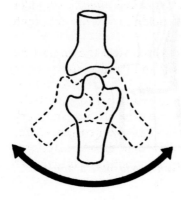

Figure 1.12 *Two bones that come together to form a joint have a certain range of movement*

this problem. Let's take a closer look at one of your joints. A joint is formed when two bones come together and are held together by ligaments. These bones have a certain range of movement (Figure 1.12). Forced movement outside this range produces 'sprain' and/or dislocation. The catch is that the joint must move through its total range of normal movement or it will tend to be limited only to the range that it is used to moving in. This law of nature says, 'If you do not use it, you will lose it!'

If you have ever broken your leg and had it in plaster, you will understand this principle. When the plaster is first removed from your leg, you can hardly move the joints. They are stiff and the muscles weak from lack of use. If you work hard to rehabilitate the leg by frequent stretching of the joint and exercising the muscles, you should regain full function of movement and strength.

You now know that your body tends to conform to the positions it assumes the most, and the body will restrict joint movement to the range that it commonly uses. It takes time for these changes to affect you because these processes of conformity and restriction progress slowly. You may not be aware of a problem until it becomes serious in terms of pain, muscle spasm, tension or fatigue, due to imbalance, misalignment, restriction and nerve irritation.

A middle-aged man consulted me one day for a neck and shoulder problem. He explained that his neck and shoulder had started to bother him several years earlier, but he hadn't thought much of it. He was an avid golfer, but swinging the clubs became painful. Instead of having his problem examined and treated, he gradually stopped playing golf. He said he had lost interest in the game because it made him uncomfortable. As time passed, other activities which involved reaching with his arms and shoulders and turning his neck bothered him, so he limited his activities still further. He finally decided to seek help when he could no longer look over his shoulder to back his car out of the drive and couldn't raise his arm high enough to apply underarm deodorant.

It took time, treatment and hard work to correct the underlying problem, which we discovered was a neck and shoulder injury from a fall he had suffered. He was ultimately able to retain over 80 per cent of the function of his neck, shoulder and arm. Along with the physical improvement was an improvement in his attitude and work productivity. This typical case illustrates how limited movement creates increasing restriction, which over time greatly interferes with body function and the ability to perform routine daily activities such as work, sleep and recreation.

Time can be a friend or an enemy. If you are not doing anything about maintaining good posture or exercising your body to keep its mobility and vitality, then time is your enemy, and you are likely to suffer the consequences in one form or another. If you strive to obtain and maintain good postural habits and keep your body and its joints flexible and properly conditioned, time can be your friend.

The advantages of sitting properly

You may be asking yourself, 'If slumping in my chair is so bad for me, why does it feel better at times?' Slumping is the body's instinctive attempt to take strain and tension away from muscles that are working to maintain prolonged positions (Figure 1.13). The problem may be a result of sitting in an ill-fitting chair, sitting too long in one position without movement, sitting in an unbalanced position, or some type of spinal misalignment or condition that is causing the muscles to work harder or become fatigued.

Poor muscle condition or tension from cumulative negative stress can also be important factors. The body tries to relieve strained muscles by slumping, placing a greater burden on the spine. Shifting the burden from the muscles to the spine creates greater pressure on the discs between the vertebrae. The normal S-shaped curve of the spine is designed to bear the weight of the body effectively, while the muscles are designed to hold and maintain the spine in this position. When these curves are altered while sitting, pressure on the discs is greatly increased. Spinal imbalance or vertebral fixation

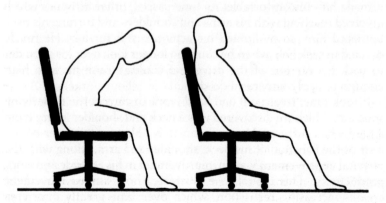

Figure 1.13 *Slumping may give short-term comfort but can cause long-term problems*

can add to disc pressures and create back problems significant enough to require professional help. Remember that physical structures bearing greater stress and strain wear out faster. In this case, your spine is more susceptible to degeneration.

Thus, long-term slumping postures can lead to significant problems which overshadow the short-term muscular relief they provide. In fact, long-term slumping ultimately requires greater muscular effort and creates increased tension and restriction of movement. You need to move about in your chair and assume various positions during the working day, and leaning forward towards your work surface is probably one of them. Acquiring the habit of slumping forward most of the time is not in your best interests. It is far better to use the contour and positioning of your chair to support your spine in an erect position and to use relaxation and exercise techniques to keep your muscles healthy. You will learn more about these techniques later in this book (see Chapter 6).

Now that you have a basic understanding of body mechanics and how your body functions, you may still be wondering what this has to do with your job. You were employed to perform certain physical and mental tasks so that your employer could provide a product or service to consumers. In the private sector, the company must produce this product or service efficiently, competitively and for a profit. Otherwise, the company or business could not exist. In the public sector, the operation should run efficiently and effectively within a restricted budget. You were chosen because your employer had confidence that you could perform certain tasks which were essential to the operation of the business or company. You should take pride in being selected for your ability to perform effectively those tasks which you were assigned.

You must, however, be able to perform your work efficiently, accurately and consistently in order to keep your employment and receive the monetary rewards and other benefits which result from your talents and services. If you and your fellow workers could not perform the designated tasks efficiently, accurately and consistently, the company or business could not thrive and you would risk losing your job.

Your ability to perform your tasks with greater comfort and ease will not only increase your productivity, but also increase your job satisfaction and make a healthier and more pleasant environment for you to work in. Less stress and strain at work preserve your energy for leisure-time enjoyment as well as your home, personal and family life.

Fit For Work

Now read on to the next chapter about your work space and learn how you can preserve your body and still perform your tasks at maximum efficiency and comfort. It is important to you!

2
Your Work Space

Your own work area

Look round your work area. What do you see? You probably have a chair, a desk, a light, possibly a computer terminal with a keyboard, a typewriter, a telephone, a calculator, pens, pencils and other tools, paper, and probably books, magazines and catalogues. You may have family pictures or personal belongings you are fond of to make your work area a little more like home. So here you are, the operator of all this. Here, you must perform efficiently tasks which are vital to the operation of the company or business. Just like the pilot of an aeroplane, you have your tools and instruments in front of you.

Figure 2.1 *Look at the equipment and materials you have in your work area and how they are arranged*

However, is your 'instrument panel' arranged properly for your body and your work?

You may have been hired to replace someone who worked in this work area before you. Suppose that person was left-handed and you are right-handed, or he was six feet one inch tall and you are five feet four inches tall. Suppose your predecessor was lazy, inefficient and left the area in a mess. You, on the other hand, want to be comfortable and productive so things will be better for you and your employer. At this point your surroundings certainly aren't going to suit you and your body. You may make some changes instinctively, but unless you know how things are supposed to fit, you may be wide of the mark and still experience some problems.

The best way to make the work area and you fit together is to look at it as though this were your first day in the job. It's like a fresh start. After all, you are gaining a different perspective about your work and it may make your job seem new again. We will start at the foundation – your chair – and work upwards.

Your chair

If you use the same chair every day, adjusting it properly to fit you may require little daily effort. If you use a different chair each day or someone else uses your chair during another shift (Figure 2.2), you need to adjust it each time you use it, as you would adjust your car seat, steering wheel and mirrors if someone else had used your car. If you don't, you and your body will pay the price over a period of time.

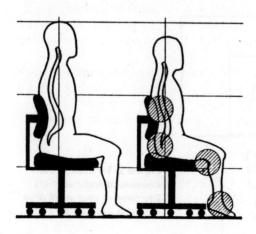

Figure 2.2 *Is your chair adjusted to fit your body?*

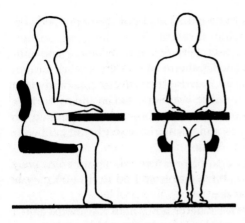

Figure 2.3 *Well-supported and balanced sitting positions*

The objective is to make your chair fit the length, size and contours of your body for maximum support and comfort. Your body, like your fingerprints, is unique and deserves a personally modified chair which will allow you to sit comfortably for many hours each day. Study the illustrations of recommended sitting postures (Figure 2.3). I might add that what is considered the perfect sitting position is not strictly defined for all humans and varies according to the type of work you do, so only the basic guidelines are illustrated here. You should use the posture or postures that make you feel most comfortable, but still provide support while you perform your tasks. Do not confuse support and comfort with thick, soft, overstuffed chairs with cushions. If you sink into your chair more than an inch your body tends to collapse into the cushions and does not get the proper support it needs. Your chair should be lightly padded so the cushion can distribute the weight of your body evenly. Fabric upholstery on the cushions helps to prevent slipping and sliding, and reduces the amount of effort required to maintain the appropriate sitting posture.

Before 1900, it was thought that the correct posture for work performed in the sitting position was in a chair which rigidly supported the spine at a right-angle to the legs, with the knees also bent at right-angles. In fact, this quickly becomes uncomfortable, and it is almost impossible to do your work in this one position. Pressure soon develops in the back, buttocks and thighs when holding this position, making it difficult to concentrate on your job. When your thighs are at right angles to your back, the curve of your lower back tends to straighten, unless you have and use a properly contoured backrest support. The usual compensation for lack of proper backrest support is to take the weight of the upper body off the lower back by slumping forward. This slumping posture increases pressure on the discs between the vertebrae and ultimately makes the muscles and ligaments of your back work harder, thus increasing the tendency towards strain. If you constantly lean to the right or to the left at work, you may also be adding further stress and strain to your body. You are now beginning to understand how the postures and positions in which you hold your body can make you uncomfortable.

You can remove a great deal of pressure and strain from your body by adjusting the backrest position and tension height, chair height and the angle of the seat.

The type of work you perform determines how you should adjust your chair (Figure 2.4). If your chair is not adjustable, get up out of it more often, say ten minutes in every hour. Also stretch more, as stresses and strains build up quickly. Do all you can to make your work area suit your physique. If the task requires reading and writing at a desk, you need to lean forward, so the seat should be tilted forward by up to 15 degrees. Your thighs will then tilt downwards, helping to preserve the natural curves of your spine and reduce the pressure on your thighs. The seat can be adjusted slightly higher when it is tilted forward. Recent studies have indicated that a slightly higher seat height may reduce disc pressures in the spine. If you primarily operate a computer terminal with a keyboard, you do not need to lean forward as much, so the seat can

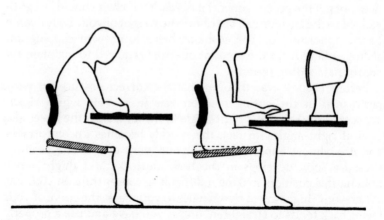

Figure 2.4 *Adjusting the chair seat may greatly improve comfort*

be tilted slightly backwards (up to 5 degrees from level) to enable you to take advantage of the lumbar support provided by the backrest.

Studies performed by Drs Grandjean, Hunting and Piderman in Zurich during 1983 revealed that most visual display unit operators preferred and used postures in which they leaned backwards in a position similar to that of a car driver. A growing number of people, however, favour seat tilting for all work-intensive tasks. Do not tilt the seat forward to such an extent that you feel you are sliding out of the chair, nor backwards so that you are uncomfortable or the edge of the seat digs into your lower thighs.

Your work surface

The height to which you adjust your chair depends on the height of your work surface, the size and shape of your body, and the nature of your task. If your task involves a computer terminal and keyboard, it is best to keep your forearms at a 75- to 90-degree angle to your upper arms (Figure 2.5). The forearms may be angled even further upwards for tasks involving a typewriter (Figure 2.6). The difference is easy to understand. The viewing screen of a computer terminal is usually several inches above the keyboard, so the hands and eyes can be further apart. On a typewriter, however, the printing of type on the paper is very close to the keys. If the forearms were at right-angles to the upper arms, you would have to lean forward frequently to look at the print. If your job involves much use of a telephone, calculator or handwriting, the elbows or forearms should be allowed to rest on the work surface. This

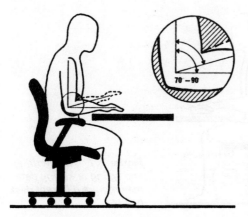

Figure 2.5 *The forearm to upper arm angle is best maintained at a 75- to 90-degree angle for computer tasks*

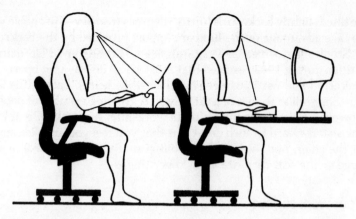

Figure 2.6 *The forearms may be angled upwards for tasks involving a typewriter*

reduces the effects of strain on the shoulders and upper body from bearing the weight and muscle activity of the arms and hands. If you make mechanical drawings, blueprints or other drawings and designs on a drafting table while sitting, the table should be angled towards you in such a way that you do not need constantly to bend your body too far forward. Tilted work surfaces are good for reading but not necessarily for handwriting tasks.

As a general rule, the closer the distance between the hands and eyes for the operation of office equipment and in carrying out other tasks, the higher the desk height should be (Figure 2.7). This is to

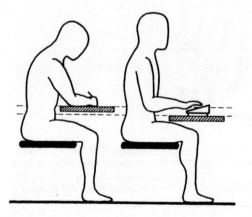

Figure 2.7 *Handwriting and typing or keying data may require different desk heights*

support the arms, hands and upper body so that the body does not have to lean with the head tilted too far forward. Remember that people using a drawing board can angle the work surface towards them, thereby reducing excessive forward bending.

Your task determines the proper height of your work surface in relation to your hands and eyes, as well as the angles of your arms, elbows, wrists and hands. A work surface height and angle which could be easily adjusted would be ideal, but most work surfaces are immobile or it is not feasible to adjust them frequently. The chair height must then be adjusted in relation to the height of the work surface in order to fit your body properly.

Your chair should be angled appropriately for your comfort and the job in question, and the chair height adjusted so that your arms, hands and upper body fit your task. Your feet need a firm foundation to relieve pressure from the legs and to maintain your body balance. If, after you have made the above changes, your legs are dangling or your feet are not firmly planted on the floor, you will need a footrest (Figure 2.8). A good footrest should be stable enough not to shift or move about when in use, wide enough to place both feet on comfortably, and have a non-skid surface. A footrest would be more comfortable if the surface were angled – up to 15 degrees – towards the toes. Be careful not to let the footrest restrict your leg movement and be careful not to trip or twist your ankle when leaving your work area.

The backrest of your chair is also very important. Take advantage

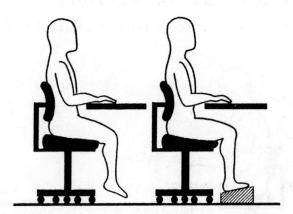

Figure 2.8 *A footrest is indicated if the feet dangle or are not firmly placed on the floor*

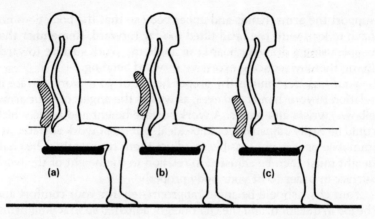

Figure 2.9 *(a) Proper backrest position (b) Backrest too high (c) Backrest too low*

of it. The backrest should arch forward to support the natural forward curve of your lower spine, but it won't work unless you use it. The idea is to support the curve of your lower back in order to divert some of the pressure from your upper body weight into the cushion. If the cushion pushes below the waistline into the sacral bone and pelvis, it is not very useful. The backrest should fit higher to support the arch of the lower back and the spot where the forward curve of the lower back changes to the backward curve of the middle back (Figure 2.9). Support in this area will help to keep the shoulders upright and reduce weight and pressure on the lower back.

Some of us have short legs, and short legs mean short thighs. If

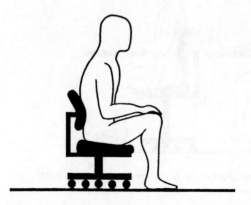

Figure 2.10 *Make sure your chair fits your body and works for you instead of against you, as in this case*

this is true for you, it may be difficult to sit far enough back to take maximum advantage of the backrest without the backs of your knees pressing into the chair edge, causing pressure and irritation. On the other hand, if you are taller and have longer than average legs, you may feel cramped in your chair and work area (Figure 2.10). If either of these is your situation, do the best you can and pay special attention to the exercises and other suggestions to reduce physical stress and strain in your work. Each of us is unique in shape and size, and we need to discover our own unique physical characteristics in order to learn how to eliminate unnecessary strain from our work. The more adjustable your work environment, the better it is for you and your productivity, but you must take the time and effort to make it conform to your special needs. Adjusting your work area to fit you should be as important as choosing clothes and shoes that fit.

A couple of important additional points about your chair need a mention. Most office chairs are able to rotate or swivel. If you need to turn from side to side to perform your tasks, this capacity to swivel is essential, but try to keep your shoulders and hips evenly aligned with each other as much as possible (Figure 2.11). Avoid extreme twisting and leaning, especially if it involves reaching for heavy objects, such as books, manuals or catalogues. Most chairs are also equipped with four or five casters which allow the chair to move easily from one place to another while you are still sitting. Here again, avoid twisting your body while pushing your chair from one place to another. Make sure the casters move properly and don't stick or lock at the wrong time.

For many, armrests are useful because they support the forearms,

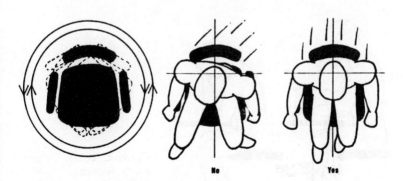

Figure 2.11 *Use the chair's ability to swivel and roll instead of twisting and bending your body to perform your tasks*

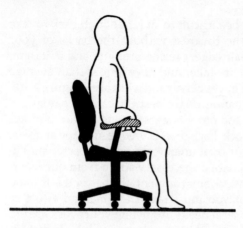

Figure 2.12 *Armrests may help to reduce muscle strain and fatigue*

and this reduces fatigue and strain on the shoulders, neck and upper body (Figure 2.12). Armrests also provide leverage or support to help a person get in and out of the chair. If the armrests restrict you in your work or are uncomfortable, they may not be practical for you. In many cases, it is simply a matter of personal preference.

Your tasks probably involve several different postures and your chair should support you in these various positions. Mr Bill Stumpf used time-lapse photography to document the movements and postures of office workers during a typical day. He used this information to help him design a better chair for office workers and the results of his study were published in 1982. Mr Stumpf isolated three basic postural patterns:

1. First is the 'work-intensive' posture. This is when you are deeply

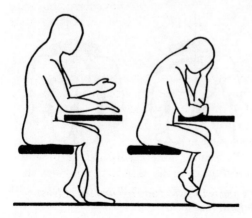

Figure 2.13 Work-intensive postures

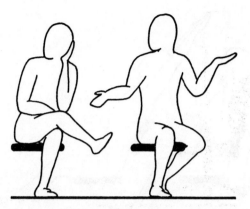

Figure 2.14 *Conversational postures*

involved in a task, such as writing, typing, drawing or assembling, and you are not consciously aware of the way you are sitting (Figure 2.13). While in a work-intensive posture you may tuck your legs under the chair and have a tendency to lean forward towards your work. Because you are involved in the task, the chair adjustments you made earlier are essential to allow the chair to support you properly. It is also important to develop the habit of keeping your lower back arched forward and reducing the forward tilt of your head during this type of activity.

2.   Next are the 'conversational' postures during which you may be reading, thinking, or talking to a fellow worker (Figure 2.14). You may shift your arms and legs frequently or turn sideways in your chair. This posture provides you with some movement, but care should be taken to ensure that your chair is still supporting your body.

3.   Last come the 'relaxation' or 'stretching' postures. When you are concentrating hard on your work, your body probably does not move very much. The build-up of tension from this stationary position needs to be released throughout the day. Use the flexibility of your chair's backrest to lean back, and take the time to stretch your hands, arms, shoulders, neck, legs and feet (Figure 2.15). It is in the reclining position that you reduce the pressure and strain on the discs of your spine and your muscles. This relaxation will clear your mind, so you will be refreshed and ready to continue your work. You may choose to stand up and walk around for a moment or two after

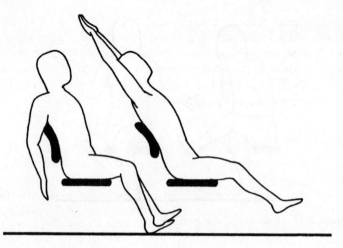

Figure 2.15 *Relaxation or stretching postures*

a period of sitting in a concentrated, work-intensive position in order to help relieve your physical tension.

Arrangement of work materials

We have already discussed the height of your work surface and some of the characteristics of tasks involving such things as computer terminals, typewriters, telephones and so on. We will talk about each of these office instruments later, but what is important here is the arrangement of the various materials on your work surface.

Let's use the airline pilot's cockpit as an illustration. The pilot sits in his or her seat with the most important item, the view of the outside world, as the main focus. The essential instruments and dials are also directly in front of the pilot, arranged round the window and within easy reach. Headphones and microphones are provided to transmit and receive verbal information. Auxiliary gauges and dials are arranged round and beside the more essential instruments. Ideally, all the vital instruments are almost at his or her fingertips. Less essential controls are strategically placed according to importance and frequency of use. The pilot does not have to twist or bend out of the seat to operate the aircraft.

Have a good look at your own personal work area. The items you use most often should be placed within easy view or access, so you will not have to twist or bend your body excessively while using them. Excessive reaching takes time and can strain your body in the sitting position, especially if it is more in one direction than the other. You should arrange the materials in your work area in their order of priority to help reduce repetitive or prolonged one-sided movements. The nature of your work determines the arrangement of the instruments, tools and materials.

Computerised work areas

Virtually every work setting which involves the use of visual display units is unique, for several reasons: work surface heights and depths vary; work areas vary according to location in the room and create different light patterns from windows, doors and overhead fixtures; our bodies vary in size and shape, so the best way for us to fit into a particular work area differs; visual display units vary in screen size and shape, according to the different manufacturers' specifications and the requirements of the tasks performed; even the size, shape and colour of the characters on the display vary. For these reasons, in addition to your own particular eyesight, it is impossible to give you an exact eye-to-screen distance. A generous range would be 14 to 30 inches, but the proper eye-to-screen distance should allow you to see all the characters on your visual display screen easily without making you bend your head and body forwards or backwards. The characters should be clear and free from visible flickering. You should be able to hold your head in a normal position and just move your eyes to see the characters at the extreme edges of the screen. One common method is to position the screen so that the centre is at about the same level as your chin (Figure 2.16). This could be a problem if the display screen and keyboard cannot be separated. Most visual display unit operators prefer screens that are tilted towards their eyes.

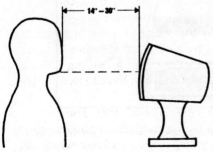

Figure 2.16 *The eye-to-screen distance may vary from 14 to 30 inches and the centre of the screen may be most comfortable at about chin level*

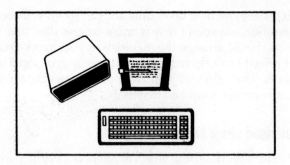

Figure 2.17 *High-frequency data entry work*

If your job involves high-frequency data entry in which you key information from hard copy (text or papers) into a computer with a visual display screen, and you use the computer screen only to check your work, the keyboard should be placed directly in front of you with the copy positioned on a stand, also in front of you (Figure 2.17). The visual display can be positioned to the side and angled towards you so that you can check your work.

If your task is to key information into the computer in order to bring up information on to the screen, and you occasionally write down some of this information, you should have the keyboard and display screen directly in front of you with paper and pencil to one side within easy reach (Figure 2.18). Be sure to leave enough space on your work surface to allow you to write comfortably and legibly.

If you usually write down information from the display screen and occasionally use the keyboard, the screen and your writing

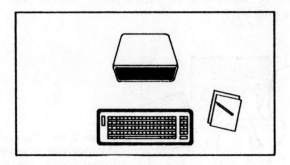

Figure 2.18 *Retrieving and manipulating information on the screen to be written down occasionally*

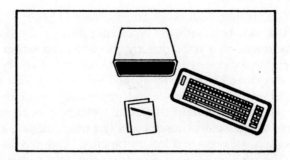

Figure 2.19 *Writing information from the screen with occasional use of the keyboard*

materials should be directly in front of you, with the keyboard conveniently placed to one side (Figure 2.19). The screen should be appropriately angled towards your field of vision.

Heavy catalogues and books should be arranged close by on the work surface in such a manner that you do not have to lift or pull them with your body in an awkward position. If you need to get a heavy volume that is not within easy reach, stand up to get it or roll your chair closer to it before attempting to lift it. Whatever you do, try to prevent excessive reaching and straining.

Non-computerised work areas

Those of you who do not use a computer terminal with keyboard

Figure 2.20 *Typing from a source document*

also need to arrange your work area in order of priority. A typist usually functions best with the typewriter directly ahead and the source document on a stand directly above the typewriter (Figure 2.20) or positioned closely to one side. Remember, if you type with your head and neck constantly turned to one side, you need to stretch and exercise your neck and upper body regularly to the opposite side. This will reduce or avoid restrictions with resultant imbalances to the spine, muscles and ligaments, accompanied by tiredness, pain, stiffness and loss of function. You may be able to alternate the position of your copy from the right to the left side every few days to help reduce the effects of one-sided activities and unbalanced postures.

You may have a telephone in your work area. Its position on your work surface will depend on how frequently you use it. Keep it within reasonable reach and if you talk on the phone while you are writing, typing or keying information, avoid clenching the receiver between your ear and shoulder (Figure 2.21). This position forces the head and neck to tilt and the shoulder muscles to tense up, causing strain and pressure to the neck and upper back vertebrae, muscles, ligaments and sensitive nerves. Excessive or prolonged misuse of this posture causes neck and shoulder strain with pain and/or numbness into the arms and hands as well as the potential for headaches. The conventional telephone receiver was designed to be hand-held, and if you use your shoulder and neck to support it, you are not using it properly. There are various attachments which allow you to use the receiver in a more appropriate manner: your

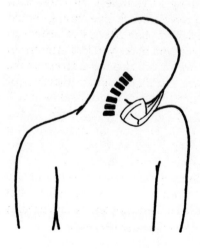

Figure 2.21 *Bracing a telephone between your head and shoulder can cause neck problems*

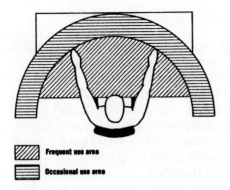

Frequent use area

Occasional use area

Figure 2.22 *Position work materials according to priority and frequency of use: high-priority area and lower-priority area*

local telephone shop, electrical goods or department store may have several solutions available.

Headphones with microphone or speaker attachments are available for those who have to use the telephone a lot in their work. Be sure to find out about any precautions regarding their long-term use which may affect your sense of hearing.

Many tasks involve the use of calculators, adding machines and other items of office equipment not mentioned, but which may be essential to your work. Use the rule of priority and frequency of use when positioning them in your work area (Figure 2.22). Take time during the appropriate breaks to relax, move and stretch those parts of your body that are restricted or tense while performing your tasks.

It is important to avoid unnecessary clutter in order to operate your work area efficiently. Everything on your desk, shelves and in your drawers should be important to your work. Everything should have a place and should be returned to its place after use. Clutter can hide important papers and messages, and make you less efficient in the performance of your duties. Clutter can also cause stress: make time now to organise your work area, using the above guidelines of priority and frequency of use. Once this is accomplished, you will feel better and it will be easier to approach your desk at the beginning of the day. Once you have got yourself organised, you must maintain the freedom from clutter. Mark down on your calendar one day each month as a 'check work areas' day.

Now you have the basics for adjusting your work area to suit you and your unique body characteristics. It takes some effort, but remember that you will be rewarded in terms of less strain, greater comfort and improved productivity and job satisfaction.

The visual display unit

Let's face it, we are riding the wave of the computer and information revolution. One of the most important aspects of this revolution is the progress and refinement of the computer with the visual display unit (VDU). The VDU has many names such as CRT (cathode ray tube), VDT (visual display terminal), terminal, screen, and so on. The explosive transition into a computer world has caused a great deal of apprehension and stress in many of our lives. Fear is born of the unknown or of misunderstanding, but our fears and anxieties cannot turn back the wave of this transition. To survive and thrive, we must live in the present and be prepared to understand and adapt to the changes that are yet to come. If you have a basic understanding of how the computer works, it may be easier for you to adjust to the information age we have entered.

Let's examine a computer from the user's point of view. The visual display unit has a keyboard which functions as a typewriter with recognisable letters, numbers and symbols. We 'communicate' with the computer by keying the correct letters, numbers or symbols into the central processing unit (CPU) or 'brain' of the computer; it searches its memory according to the way its current program was designed in order to put the information we want on the display screen. The challenge is to enter commands in the exact language that the computer understands so as to get the information we need. We can also enter data to be stored for future use. This is an oversimplification, of course, but this is essentially what the computer does. It will only perform the functions for which it is programmed, and its performance will depend on our understanding of the machine and its particular program. It was built as a timesaver and aid to mankind.

To become a successful and effective computer operator, you will need to understand how to tell the computer what functions you want it to perform. When you first sit in front of a computer terminal and a keyboard, you may find it alarming. This is a normal reaction because it is new to you. The computer terminal is an item of office equipment much like a typewriter, but it is more complex: with a typewriter, you press a key and a symbol is printed; with a computer terminal, you press a key and a great deal of information may be displayed on the screen, or manipulated in some other way. You must understand that the computer is acting in accordance to the way it was programmed, in the same way that the typewriter was built to respond on a key-by-key basis.

Stress generated by working with a computer can be eased if you consider that it simply responds to your commands in accordance with its program and memory. Once you realise this, and thoroughly understand how to send information to the computer in the language it understands enabling it to carry out your commands, you will have taken a major step towards learning to relax while operating the VDU.

3
Your Office Environment

Many factors in your work environment directly affect your body and your ability to concentrate on your job. When you are hard at work, it is best for you and your job performance if distractions are minimal. When you are able to keep your attention and concentrate fully on your duties, you are operating at maximum efficiency. This allows you to work faster, and with greater accuracy and consistency. It also makes you and your employer happier. It makes your employment secure, and thus provides for you and your family.

With this in mind, your goal is to become more aware of factors in the work environment that can be distracting and how you can deal with them. This knowledge will lead to greater comfort, less stress, increased productivity and job satisfaction.

General lighting considerations

Approximately 85 per cent of the information you receive from your environment is gathered through your eyes. Proper lighting is therefore high on the list of priorities for a good work environment. Without proper lighting, you may not be able to see your work easily. General lighting or lighting for specific tasks should enable you to concentrate your vision on your work without distraction.

If your job is primarily concerned with printed, handwritten or other materials that do not involve the use of a computer terminal with a visual display screen, the lighting should be bright enough for you to see and use your materials easily. Inadequate lighting makes it difficult for your eyes to focus on the materials and objects. It takes

Figure 3.1 *Direct light from windows or lamps can interfere with your vision*

more time for the appropriate information to be deciphered by the brain and for you to perform your work. This extra effort can cause tiredness as well as eye strain. As the day goes on, it becomes more difficult and tiresome for you to get on with your work.

General room lighting in this instance should not be so bright that you have to squint. Avoid interference with your field of vision by direct light from windows or lamps while working (Figure 3.1). Reflections on your desk from strong direct light can also interfere with your ability to see and use your work materials. The cumulative effects of continually squinting to avoid bright lights or reflections can cause or contribute to eye strain and headaches. Subconsciously shifting your body, neck and head to avoid bright lights or reflections can cause enough stress and strain to produce or aggravate other symptoms such as neck pain, back pain, muscle tension and fatigue.

Computer terminal lighting

A computer terminal with a visual display screen combines a typewriter and a television screen with the principles of electronics and magnetics. Similar to a television screen, the VDU emits light from the screen like a flashlight. When viewing the screen from your work area you will notice that it has a reflective quality like a mirror (Figure 3.2). The characteristics of lighted symbols on a mirror-like screen make it difficult to place a VDU in an office that had previously been used only for typing and similar tasks without special considerations.

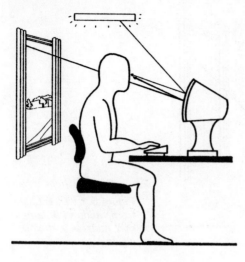

Figure 3.2 *Reflections on a visual display screen can interfere with your ability to see characters on the screen easily*

A VDU emits light, so a lower level of light is needed in this part of the workplace. In addition, the screen has a quality that reflects direct room lights into the operator's eyes causing 'blind spots' to appear on the screen. A lower level of light or a different quality of overhead lighting or light fixtures may make it easier to see the numbers and characters on the screen. Even the light from windows, light-coloured walls, or images from pale clothing may appear as reflections on the screen and interfere with your view of the letters and symbols. You may have to screw up your eyes or crane your neck in order to avoid the reflections or glare. These actions produce strain on your eyes, cause headaches, neck pain or other symptoms, and can slow down your work as well as reduce your accuracy and consistency. If you are constantly endeavouring to avoid these problems, your tasks become less enjoyable.

Room temperaure and draughts

What is considered the most comfortable room temperature varies somewhat from person to person. Some of us are more heat sensitive, others are more cold sensitive. It is difficult to set the temperature in a room where a number of people have to work so that all are completely comfortable. There are, however, several things you can do to make the temperature more suitable for your body.

If you sit next to a window and the sun shines in, making you too

Figure 3.3 *Windows can magnify the sun's heat and make you quite uncomfortable*

warm (Figure 3.3), you can pull down the blinds to divert sunlight and heat. Blinds or curtains may also be pulled down to prevent or reduce the chill from windows during cold weather.

Look up at the ceiling or down to the floor to locate the heat or, if your office has air conditioning, air conditioning vents. Forced air, whether it is warm or cool, can affect your comfort as well as your muscles. For example, if an air conditioning vent is located above you and blows out cool air, the muscles beneath the skin that are exposed to this draught may become tense (Figure 3.4). Your body tissues

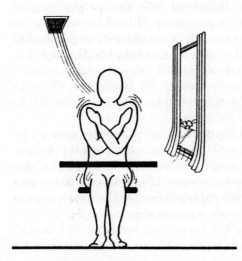

Figure 3.4 *Air conditioning vents can cause distracting draughts*

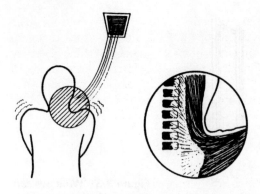

Figure 3.5 *Cool air that blows directly on to the neck increases muscle tension*

respond to temperature changes in the same way as the pavement in front of your house or flat. When it is hot, it expands; when it is cold, it contracts. If cool air blows directly on one side of your neck, those muscles will tend to become tense (Figure 3.5). This may create a muscular imbalance or tension which can pull spinal vertebrae out of alignment or create spasm which may irritate the nerves that cause or contribute to ailments such as headaches, neck pain, back pain and shoulder and arm discomfort.

This reminds me of a patient I was treating for headaches. We determined that muscle tension on the right side of his neck had caused vertebral restriction and spasm, creating nerve irritation that caused the headaches. He would always obtain relief after treatment, but within a short period the headaches would return. Upon further investigation, we discovered that this patient enjoyed sleeping with the sound of a fan running. During the summer, he would place the fan on the right side of his bed and direct it to blow over his body so as to avoid having to use his air conditioning. The cool breeze from the fan created muscle tension which created a chain reaction that ultimately caused his headaches. Once he eliminated this cool draught, our treatment was successful, and he was relieved of his severe headaches.

Cool air movements and draughts are very common, so check for these in your workplace, as well as at home. Correcting the problem may be as easy as having an air vent diverted so it will not blow directly on to your body. If you are unusually sensitive to hot or cold, it is important that you dress appropriately for the conditions you will be exposed to in your work environment.

Another important consideration in room temperature is humidity, which is the amount of moisture in the air. If the humidity is too high or too low, it can make the temperature feel warmer or cooler than it really is. The effect on your body is the important factor to consider. Larry Whitehead, an industrial hygienist at the University of Michigan, found that ideally a room should have a humidity level of between 40 and 60 per cent. Some computers and office equipment require lower humidity levels, but the closer to the 40 to 60 per cent range, the more comfortable most of us will feel.

Noise

Many of us are distracted by noise (Figure 3.6). Certain noises produced by machines, air conditioning vents, background music and voices may distract you and interfere with your concentration. Remember, you were hired to perform certain tasks to help your business or company function, and distractions can reduce your ability to do your work efficiently.

The noise of equipment can sometimes be reduced with proper maintenance or by contacting the equipment dealers or manufacturers to see what can be done about any loud, irritating or distracting sounds that may be a problem. A telephone ring can be controlled by adjusting the volume control, usually located on the side or the bottom of the telephone. If there are many telephones in an office, the ringing can be very distracting. However, make sure you do not turn the volume down so low that you miss any calls when you are away from your desk. Other distracting noises and the sound of

Figure 3.6 *Distracting noises can interfere with your concentration as you perform your tasks*

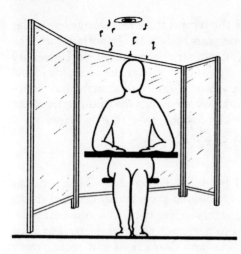

Figure 3.7 *A possible solution to noise problems is specially padded partitions*

voices can be reduced with specially padded individual partitions (Figure 3.7), if practical and feasible. You must learn what is most comfortable and best for you and work within that framework. Loss of hearing can also be stressful and affect your job performance, so don't hesitate to go for a hearing test if you feel this may be a problem.

You now have a better idea of how you interact with your environment, and you have learned some ways in which you can change your environment to your greater comfort, and to help you to perform your tasks more productively. We now have the momentum to carry us through the rest of this book, so let's look at the common physical problems that people experience in occupations which require sitting, and some suggestions which will help you to deal with these problems, or better still, prevent them from happening.

4

Common Physical Complaints

Pain, restriction of movement, fatigue and the stress these symptoms produce may be among the most prominent factors which limit productivity, accuracy, consistency, job satisfaction and morale. These factors are often the reason why many workers leave their jobs. You are not alone if you suffer from some or all of these symptoms. They are indicators of a problem, and you should do what you can to reduce or eliminate them in your life, for the consequences of suffering are too great. In addition, problems that are dealt with in their early stages are usually much easier to correct than if they are allowed to progress to a more serious state.

How injuries occur

It is a myth to believe that injuries and problems develop in the nerve, muscle, ligament and skeletal systems by over-exertion or improper lifting alone. Physical injuries, like sprains and strains, usually arise in one of two ways. Most people think that more injuries result from improper lifting, extreme physical exertion (Figure 4.1), from a trauma such as a fall or car accident, but more than half do not. In this type of problem, a huge force is exerted on the muscles, tendons, ligaments or bones over a short period of time, causing strain, sprain, tearing of the supportive tissues and maybe even bone fracture. Pain and swelling soon develop, and you would quickly know that you have been injured.

Another mechanism for injury is when less forceful pressure is applied to parts of the body by improper movements over a longer

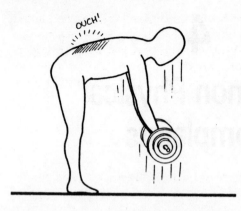

Figure 4.1 *Injuries can be caused by improper lifting or extreme physical exertion over a short period of time*

period or by many repetitions (Figure 4.2). This produces abnormal changes in the structures of the body and you may not have an immediate sprain or swelling as when experiencing a sudden, violent trauma. Pain and other symptoms will develop gradually and you may not take the appropriate action to remedy the problem. You may not even know where or how the problem developed, unless you are aware of the way your body works and how slowly problems can develop.

The good news is that you have already read this far and that means that you care enough about yourself to want to feel better, and you care enough about your job to want to perform your tasks

Figure 4.2 *Physical problems can also be caused by less forceful but improper movements over a long period or by many repetitions*

more effectively. Since you have already read and learned about your body and how it works, you will begin to take action to investigate and remedy the problem. You have learned that sudden, excessive forces over a short period of time and slow, repetitious forces over a longer period can cause you physical strain and sprain, which will result in painful, often disabling, symptoms.

Caution

The symptoms described here are commonly experienced among office and industrial workers as well as the general public. Suggestions for taking action to reduce or eliminate these common complaints must not be construed as a substitute for appropriate professional care. If you have recurrent problems that are not helped by changes to your work environment or the other suggestions outlined in this book, you should seek professional advice. If you have any questions about the suggestions made in this book, take them and the book to a qualified and trusted professional. There is no substitute for person-to-person care.

Other causes of physical symptoms

One additional point to be made before we talk about the common symptoms is that the physical complaints you may have at work are not necessarily caused by your job alone. Previous injuries to your body may surface or be aggravated by prolonged sitting or other factors while performing office duties. For instance, if you suffered a whiplash injury in a car accident or if you slipped on the ice during the winter and injured your lower back, your injuries are much more prone to being aggravated by occupational strain (Figure 4.3). Therefore, if you begin to experience neck pain, headaches or low back pain, and you believe it is due to all the sitting you are doing, you must realise that the injury you sustained several years before could still be affecting you. The pain becomes more apparent now because you are placing different stresses on your body These problems may require professional attention in addition to the conservative measures suggested in this book. The same applies to previous shoulder, arm, hip or leg injuries. If this is your situation, be sure to tell your doctor the full details of any previous injuries so he or she will understand your current difficulties better.

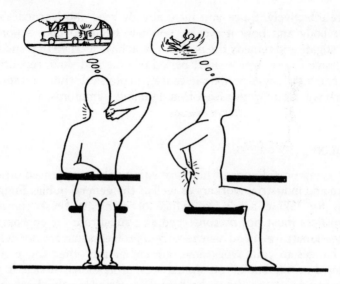

Figure 4.3 *Previous injuries may surface or be aggravated by sedentary occupations*

Eye strain

Office and sedentary occupations usually involve a great deal of reading or studying and are therefore visually demanding. There is no indication that visually demanding work in itself damages the retina of the eye. Visually intensive work does, however, pose a special challenge to the lens and the internal and external muscles of the eyeball.

The more stress and strain you place on one part of your body, the better care you must take of that part. Most of us use our eyes almost every waking moment, and this does not cause any particular problems. If, however, you focus and concentrate on small print or objects for long periods, you are not using your full range of vision. The muscles that help to focus the lens and hold the eye in a steady position will become strained and tired if held at one depth of focus for a long time, day after day. Your eyes need frequent breaks to minimise this strain. This means that you should frequently take a few moments to focus on an object far away. Look at the other end of the room or out of the window to change your depth of vision (Figure 4.4). This also helps to exercise and maintain flexibility of the lens and eye muscles. Take the time to roll and turn your eyes to the

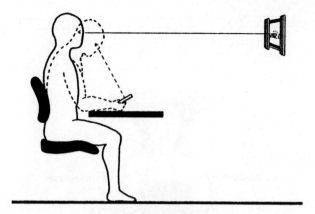

Figure 4.4 *Change your field of vision frequently by focusing on a far away object*

extremes of right and left, up and down, as well as diagonally upwards and downwards (Figure 4.5). This activity exercises the muscles that move the eyeball. These muscles obey the same rules as those that apply to your neck and back muscles. If you hold them in one position for a long time, they become tired. If the eyeball and lens muscles are subjected to this type of force, eye strain develops. This interferes with your concentration and affects your job performance and well-being. Don't let it happen to you.

If you operate a visual display unit, the light-emitting characteristics, along with the reflective quality of the screen, may pose special challenges. Glare and reflection on the screen on your desk top or the walls may interfere with your ability to see the numbers, letters and symbols easily on the screen. Under these circumstances, you may develop eye strain, and you may have to crane your neck or otherwise distort your body to avoid the glare or reflections (Figure

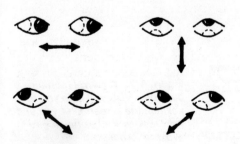

Figure 4.5 *Exercise the muscles that move the eyeball frequently*

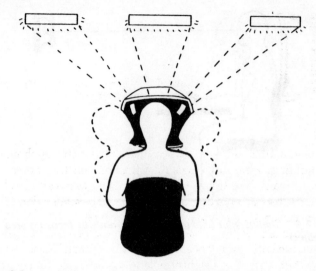

Figure 4.6 *Looking through or around screen reflections may increase eye strain as well as make you twist and turn your back and neck*

4.6). This extra physical effort inhibits your concentration and puts additional strain on your body. You may want to tilt or rotate the screen or take steps to reduce the reflection and glare.

A relatively inexpensive device, such as a swivel monitor base (Figure 4.7), can make it possible for you to tilt and rotate the position of the screen easily many times a day as light sources change. Filter and glare-reduction screens (Figure 4.8) are also available and can help in many cases. (However, they can be counter-productive if they interfere with the clarity of the characters on your screen.)

You may be able to compensate for a small amount of excessive or inadequate lighting by adjusting the brightness control knob on your screen. This is not the ideal solution: it is better to correct the

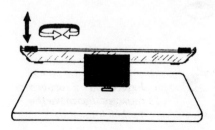

Figure 4.7 *A swivel monitor base on a VDU will help you to position the screen to fit you and your task as well as helping to avoid reflections*

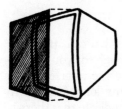

Figure 4.8 *Glare-reduction screens can be effective against reflections*

problem at source, whether it is in the light fixtures or the general inside lighting, windows, doors or reflections on the screen, work surface or walls. The brightness and contrast between the characters and the background on the screen should be adjusted so that the characters are read easily without interference.

Flickering or indistinct characters on the screen can be annoying and interfere with your concentration and comfort. These problems mean either that the brightness and contrast settings are not properly adjusted or that the VDU itself needs some maintenance.

People who wear glasses may also need to overcome special challenges. If you have bifocals or trifocals and you enter printed information into a computer, you may be looking up and down from the copy to the computer screen many times. This not only contributes to eye strain, but if you have to tilt your head back constantly in order to focus on the screen, you may develop neck, upper back and shoulder problems and so-called tension headaches (Figure 4.9). If you are in this situation, then adjusting the height of the screen, your work surface or chair height is certainly in order. You may need to consult an optician. Special computer glasses are available, if needed. A special coating can be applied to the glasses you use at work to reduce eye strain arising from the special light and reflective characteristics of computer screens.

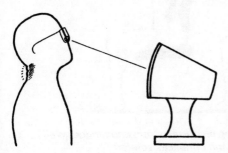

Figure 4.9 *Tilting your head backwards to view the screen through bifocals or trifocals can cause neck and upper back problems*

Back pain

Back pain is one of the most common problems that can affect you at work, as well as at home. It can be severe enough for you to have to take time off from work or annoying enough to interfere with your concentration and your ability to sit for long enough to perform your tasks efficiently. Several studies indicate that there is greater strain to the lower spine while sitting than while standing or bending. In fact, higher levels of degeneration of the bones, discs, muscles and ligaments or the lower back have been noted in a study group of sedentary workers than in a group of workers who handle heavy materials.

It is hard to wake up in the morning with enthusiasm if you know you are going to experience pain. This doesn't have to be the case: the purpose of this book is to help you to understand fully the effects that sitting has on your back, and to provide you with information that will help you to reduce unnecessary pressure and stress on your body. It is important to seek professional help in cases of persistent or recurrent pain.

The main objective is to allow your chair to support your body properly while you are sitting at your job (Figure 4.10). The idea behind a well-designed chair is for it to support the curves of the body and allow you to move into different positions as your tasks dictate. The chair should allow you to move, stretch and relax your body as needed.

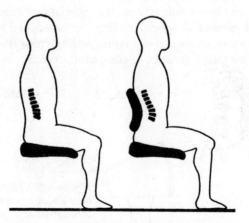

Figure 4.10 *Unsupported sitting increases strain and fatigue. Well-supported sitting reduces strain and enhances comfort*

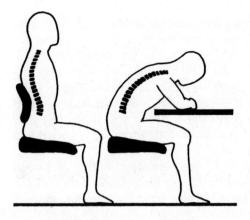

Figure 4.11 *Using the chair's support and proper posture reduce strain and pressure on the spine. Slumping increases spinal strain and pressures*

While you are sitting, the forward curve of your lower back should be supported in the proper position, and there should be even pressure on your sitting bones (ischial tuberosities). Your thighs should be comfortably situated so that the edge of the chair does not dig into your hamstring muscles. Your feet should be comfortably planted on the floor or footrest. In this position, the upper back becomes erect and your posture is good. The chair is supporting you and your spine. Slumping forward over your work (Figure 4.11) takes some of the strain from the muscles, but when your lower spine bends backwards, there is greater pressure on the cushion-like discs between the vertebrae. The slumped posture creates a chain

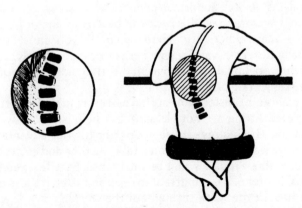

Figure 4.12 *Constant one-sided body twisting can create muscular and spinal imbalance with its undesirable effects*

61

reaction that can set the stage for spinal instability, producing nerve irritation and dangerous pressure on the discs. If this happens day after day, it would explain why you may be uncomfortable. If you are constantly twisting to one side, uneven pressure is affecting your body and the above problems will be magnified (Figure 4.12).

You can see that this is a very undesirable situation, so it is important that you make your chair work for you. It must fit your unique body properly and you must work with it to get what you want . . . comfort and support.

Let's learn what happens to your muscles during prolonged sitting activities. Muscles are bundles of long slender cells that can contract or relax to move bones. With a steady contraction, muscles hold bones in a certain position. If you are not using your chair to help support your spine in its normal position or your posture is bad, the muscles are required to take over the burden of supporting your body. When a muscle is required to maintain its contraction for prolonged periods, it requires extra effort which burns more energy and creates more waste products which the body must dispose of. It is similar to the way a fire creates heat (energy), but leaves smoke and ashes (waste). The waste products of muscle contraction must be carried away by the circulatory system, but when muscles are tensed for long periods, the blood vessels inside are compressed so they cannot carry away all the waste products.

Under these circumstances the waste products, which are irritating chemicals, build up inside the muscle and make it stay tense, as well as irritating the nerves within and around the muscle. If the tense muscle is attached to the spine, it can pull and tug, creating vertebral instability, abnormal joint motion, pressure and nerve irritation. Day after day, this cycle can be a major factor in the back pain you may experience. Here again, if you must twist or continually turn one way for long periods or repetitiously, you may be creating an imbalance between the two sides of your body, compounding your problems.

The pain and tension you suffer as the result of improper or unsupported sitting are not pleasant, but help is on the way. You have learned that you must use your chair to your advantage, and now you are learning that you must take the time and effort to relax and stretch those muscles that become tense. Specific exercises are given in Chapter 6. It is important to relax and stretch those muscles and do most of the work throughout the working day. If you take care of them, they will help to take care of you.

Neck pain

Neck and upper back pains are almost as common as low back pain. Though the neck does not bear the weight of the entire body as the lower back does, it holds up the head. The upper back must bear the weight of and support the shoulders and arms. A great deal of strain can be applied to these areas if precautions are not taken.

The head may weigh eight to fourteen pounds, and is supported by seven small vertebrae in the neck which are designed to curve forward when you are looking straight ahead (Figure 4.13). But you cannot always look straight ahead when performing your tasks. Most of the time you probably tilt your head forwards towards your work surface, with your chin slightly tucked into your chest. In this position the ligaments connecting the neck vertebrae stretch at the back and gather together at the front. The muscles in the back of your neck, shoulders and upper body tense to keep your head from falling too far towards your chest, and some of the front neck muscles tense when the head is forward. This position is within the normal range of motion for the neck and head, but if it is held too long or too frequently without taking measures to reduce or counteract the strain, the normal forward curve of the neck can become abnormally straight or even reversed. If not counteracted, the ligaments and connective tissues of the neck vertebrae will tend to conform to the positions in which the neck and head are continually held.

Prolonged or repetitious forward head tilting or one-sided head

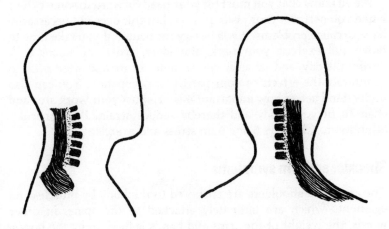

Figure 4.13 *The neck curve is designed to bow forward*

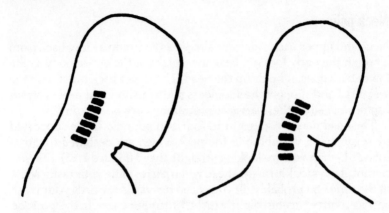

Figure 4.14 *Forward head tilting or twisting changes the neck curve*

and neck turning (Figure 4.14) can cause extra pressure on the shock-absorbing discs between the vertebrae. Locking or fixation of one or more of the joints in the neck and irritation of the nerves that leave the spinal cord from between the vertebrae can be the result. Over a long period, the discs may degenerate and arthritis develop. Nerve irritation causes pain: nerves that leave the lower neck travel to the shoulders, arms and hands. If these nerves are irritated at the neck, you may experience pain, stiffness or numbness in your shoulders, arms or hands. Nerve irritation and muscle tension at the upper neck and base of the skull may also cause headaches.

We all know that you must tilt your head forward to some extent when you perform your tasks at work, but this does not necessarily have to cause problems. It will be to your benefit if you take time to move and exercise your neck, shoulders, arms and upper back during the day, and set aside special time before and after work to counteract the effects of your particular occupation. You can also understand better how important it is to adjust your work area and chair to fit your body and thereby reduce strain. Pay particular attention to Chapters 5 and 6 on stress and exercise.

Shoulder and arm symptoms

The arms and shoulders are anchored to the body by muscles and ligaments which are ultimately attached to the spine. In other words, the weight of the arms and hands is held up by the bones, muscles and ligaments of the upper back. If you hold your arms and

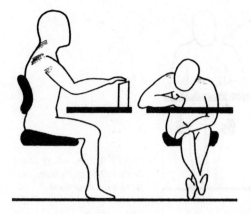

Figure 4.15 *Arm positions and work postures can cause shoulder and back problems*

hands in unrelaxed, unsupported or awkward positions while performing your tasks, you may feel the effects, not only in your arms and hands, but also in your neck, upper back and even in your lower back (Figure 4.15).

If you use a computer keyboard or a typewriter frequently, it is usually better to keep your elbows close to your body. This reduces muscle strain on the upper body. If this is not practical, you may need to rest your elbows on an armrest, if available, or rest your forearms or wrists on the desk top. Sharp or right-angled edges on work surfaces that press into the muscles, tendons and blood vessels of the forearms and wrists can cause problems, so you need to make sure that this does not apply to you. Rounded or padded edges are helpful, but you should not put pressure on your forearms or wrists to bear the weight of your upper body. It is more practical and safer to adjust your work area to fit your body, rather than trying to adjust your body to fit the work area.

If you do much handwriting and sit with one arm and elbow spread over your work surface with the other arm at your side, your body is twisted towards your work surface. This position will become tiresome and cause problems. Try to align your hips and chair with your shoulders to reduce the twisting and strain on your back, neck and shoulders (Figure 4.16). Take the necessary steps to stretch and exercise those parts of your body that become tight and strained in work positions.

Remember, previous injuries to your neck, back, shoulders, elbows, arms, wrists and hands may interfere with your comfort and ability to perform your tasks. If this is the case or you have persistent problems, seek professional guidance.

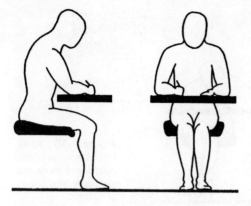

Figure 4.16 *Align your body with your chair, your desk and your task*

Wrist, hand and finger symptoms

Wrist, hand or finger pain, numbness or tingling can pose a threat to your ability to perform your office tasks. Your wrists and hands are as unique as the rest of your body. In fact, if you compare your hands to those of your fellow workers, you may discover that there is a notable difference in size and shape – yet you may be using the same office equipment. Proper positioning of your wrists and hands is very important in order to be comfortable at work.

The wrists and hands should be used in what is known as the 'neutral position' as much as possible (Figure 4.17). In this position, the wrist is not bent forwards, backwards, inwards or outwards. Extremes in any of these positions can put strain on the joints in the wrist and pressure on the tendons, blood vessels and nerves passing through the wrists. These abnormal positions also place strain on

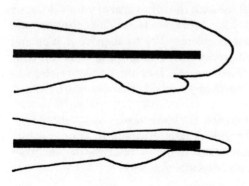

Figure 4.17 *The neutral position for wrists and hands*

Figure 4.18 *Tilt the keyboard to suit your hands and wrists*

the forearm muscles and the upper arms and shoulders which are anchored to the upper body and neck.

The keys on a computer keyboard, typewriter or calculator should be positioned so that your fingers can reach and press them easily and efficiently. If you have long hands and fingers, you may feel crowded in your ability to press the keys, which will cause your finger joints to bend and wrists extend towards you. You can reduce the strain of this awkward position by adjusting the keyboard to a more horizontal position (parallel with the work surface), as long as it does not put your arms or shoulders in a strained position. For those of you with short hands and fingers, a higher angle on the keyboard, typewriter or calculator will make the keys easier to reach (Figure 4.18). Here, again, you must be able to keep your wrists in the 'neutral position' and avoid putting strain on your forearms, upper arms, shoulders and upper back.

If you keep your wrists and hands in a constant position while performing your tasks, it is essential for you to stretch and exercise them periodically throughout the working day and during your off-duty hours. Stretching exercises after or before work are to your advantage and can reduce or counteract the effects of chronic strain. Some inflammatory and arthritic conditions make it difficult or painful to stretch and exercise these joints, so seek professional guidance if this is the case for you.

Make sure you flex and extend your fingers frequently. You should also make sure your wrists get proper exercise by flexing and extending the hand at the forearm and from side to side (Figure 4.19). The wrist does not have much movement from side to side so don't be alarmed if it feels somewhat restricted. Unaccustomed or new activities of the wrists, hands, fingers or arms can result initially in mild discomfort. Strain, pain or numbness which persist for more than two to three weeks suggests the need to make further

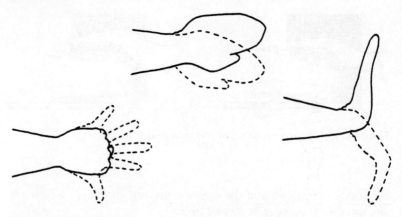

Figure 4.19 *Normal movements of the wrists and hands*

adjustments to your work area or to consult a doctor who specialises in this type of disorder.

Wrist and forearm rests can be improvised for use in the workplace (Figure 4.20), and they may be helpful as long as the hands, wrists or forearms are not strained or made to bear the weight of the upper body. Be particularly careful to avoid compressing parts of the fingers, hands, wrists, forearms, elbows or upper arms that may press into your work area or office equipment while you do your job.

Some of your leisure activities can also contribute to wrist, hand and finger problems. Riding a bicycle with your wrists extended or lifting weights with your wrists, hands, elbows or shoulders in a strained position can aggravate the symptoms you experience at work. Take a close look at your activities and postures both at work and away from work.

Figure 4.20 *Avoid letting your forearms press into the sharp edges of work surfaces. Wrist and forearm rests could be helpful*

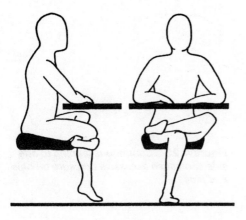

Figure 4.21 *Improper leg and foot positions can cause or contribute to leg and foot symptoms*

Leg and foot symptoms

Leg and foot problems may be less publicised, occurring less frequently than backaches, headaches and tiredness, but they certainly pose a threat to your well-being (Figure 4.21). As far as your work area is concerned, if the seat of your chair is raised too high for your legs so that your feet are not firmly planted on the floor or footrest, there may be too much pressure on the back of your thighs and the sitting bones of your pelvis (Figure 4.22). This extra pressure can impede blood flow to the legs as well as stretch and irritate some of the long nerves from your spine which pass through the back of your legs to your feet. The result can be cramping, pain or numbness in your thighs, calves or feet. This

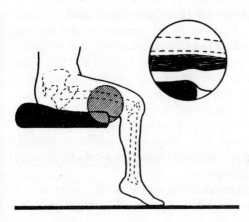

Figure 4.22 *The seat angle and chair height should be adjusted to reduce pressure on the thighs from the seat edge*

69

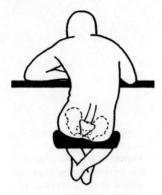

Figure 4.23 *Continuous leaning to one side can cause excessive pressure on hips and legs*

discomfort can make you restless in your chair, and you may feel the need to squirm and twist about in an attempt to become more comfortable. This discomfort can interfere with your concentration.

Your chair height should help to fit your body to your work surface. If it doesn't, it may be forcing you to lean towards or away from the desk. You can help to compensate for this by tilting the seat backwards or forwards according to your task (as discussed in Chapter 2). A well-designed chair has a seat with a rounded front edge to reduce thigh pressure. The angle of the seat should allow the long bones of the thighs to be parallel with it.

Excessive pressure on one hip or leg can be produced by leaning continuously to one side in your chair (Figure 4.23). This abnormal position is usually caused by the constant need to turn in one particular direction to perform your tasks. It is important to arrange your desk, materials and equipment so you can sit in a comfortable, balanced position.

If you carry a wallet or notebook in your back pocket, extra pressure can be applied to that hip or leg and can crowd nerves, create muscle imbalance, reduce blood circulation and tip your pelvis so that it becomes tilted or twisted (Figure 4.24). This distortion shifts your lower back off-centre, creating an imbalance and extra work for the muscles of the lower back, resulting in spinal instability. The thickness of your wallet, notebook or other items may not seem much, but if they are in your back pocket day after day and you sit for many hours each day, the problem will be magnified. This is especially important if you are travelling in a vehicle, because vibration compounds the problem.

The blood vessels in the legs are a long way from the heart, which is the major pump of the circulatory system. The heart muscles

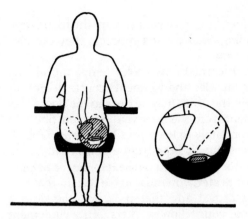

Figure 4.24 *Wallets or notebooks in a back pocket can cause a tilt in the hips or lower back as well as interfering with circulation*

contract to force blood from the heart through the arteries so that the blood can flow throughout the body and nourish all the cells. But the heart needs help to push the blood into and back out of the legs. Muscle contractions and movement of the legs help to make this circulation easier. It is clear that if you sit for long hours with your thighs and buttocks pressed into a chair or your legs knotted together under it, the leg muscles cannot help your circulation. Sitting with your legs crossed at the knees or with one foot tucked under your buttocks also interferes with the circulation and can cause nerve irritation along with ligament, muscle and joint strain in the lower back, hips, legs and feet. You need to stretch and move your legs while sitting and to get up from your chair and walk about during breaks.

Large nerves coming from the lower back run down the entire length of your legs to the tips of your toes. Nerve irritation from instability in the lower back can also cause leg, ankle and foot problems. If you have persistent back, leg, ankle or foot problems, you have made the necessary adjustments at work and have a well-designed supportive chair, you should seek professional advice to see if you have some other condition that requires attention.

Cramping, pain or numbness in the ankles, feet and arches can be the result of the situations described above, but they can also be caused or aggravated by poorly fitting or improperly designed shoes, as well as fallen or strained arches. Well-designed and professionally fitted shoes with adequate arch supports are important – not so much when you are sitting, but as you walk about at work, on your way to and from work and during your leisure activities. Make sure you do not neglect this important part of your body. Problems here may affect not only your feet, but, since your feet are the foundation of your body while standing, walking and running, they can also affect your legs, hips and back.

Earlier in this book you learned how cooler temperatures and draughts can make your muscles and ligaments contract. Hot air rises, so the coolest place in the office may be close to the floor. This cool air or the air movement from the floor vent may contribute to leg problems. Dress appropriately to keep your legs comfortable. It may be possible to redirect the air flow from a floor vent. If you know cold air is a problem for your legs, a fan heater may be helpful. If you feel that you need a heater, you must make certain that you have your employer's approval and that it is not placed in a hazardous position for you, your fellow workers, office equipment and wiring.

Headaches

What a stressful and common problem headaches are! In fact, 73 per cent of people surveyed in a recent poll said they experienced headaches. That's almost three out of four people, so if you fall into this category, you are certainly not alone (Figure 4.25).

There are many causes for the pain that you may feel anywhere from the base of your skull up to your temples, forehead, eyes and cheeks. Among the causes are nerve irritation in the neck, muscle tension, high blood pressure, eye strain, jaw joint problems, stress, sinus problems, ear problems, blood sugar problems – and so the list goes on. Science has recognised about 200 separate types and causes of headaches. Headaches are a complex health disorder requiring careful evaluation and consideration. All recurrent headaches

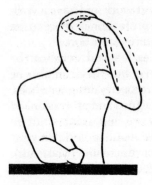

Figure 4.25 *Headaches affect nearly three out of four people*

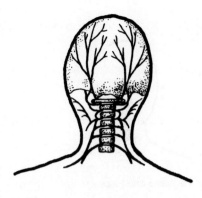

Figure 4.26 *Nerves emerging from the neck vertebrae are wrapped around the skull*

should be investigated by a competent professional who may perform tests and examinations to find out the probable cause and nature of the pain. Fortunately, most headaches are not the result of serious disease.

Let's consider how your work can cause or contribute to headaches. It is a problem to be reckoned with because headaches, like back and neck pain, can interfere with your ability to concentrate on your job, as well as affecting the satisfaction you feel from doing your job well.

First and probably foremost in office work is the complaint of the common 'tension' headache. The brain is situated inside the skull, but most of the nerves that are wrapped round the head come from the base of the skull and upper neck (Figure 4.26). The weight of your head is supported by seven small neck vertebrae which are held together by ligaments and muscles. These muscles and ligaments are strong enough to support the head on top of the neck vertebrae, yet flexible enough to allow you to turn and rotate your head. Work positions which cause prolonged tension on the neck muscles can tug and pull on the vertebrae in a way that can create spasm or instability in the vertebrae, which may cause pressure and irritation of the blood vessels and nerves of the head, thus giving you pain.

Every minute that your head is away from what is called the 'neutral position' (Figure 4.27), opposing groups of neck and upper back muscles must tense or relax in an effort to hold the weight of your head within the centre of gravity. If you hold your head forwards with your chin towards your chest, your neck and upper back muscles are working hard to keep your head from falling too far forward, and the usual forward bend of the curve in your neck is reduced, or in some cases, reversed. Holding this position for long

73

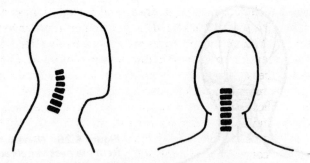

Figure 4.27 *The neutral position for the head and neck*

periods, day after day, without giving the strained muscles and ligaments the relaxation and movement they need, can cause the neck vertebrae to become misaligned which creates nerve irritation and causes pain (Figure 4.28).

If you wear bifocals or trifocals and you have to tilt your head backwards to see your computer terminal or typewriter, the joints at the back of the neck can get jammed together, resulting in nerve irritation that causes headaches or neck pain. Uncorrected vision

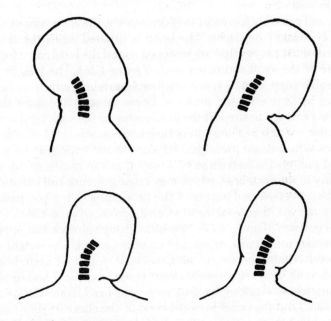

Figure 4.28 *Changing the head position alters the neck curve*

problems including nearsightedness and farsightedness can make you lean forwards or backwards in your chair in order to focus on your work. Your sitting postures may be adversely affected, causing strain and tension that result in unpleasant symptoms. Office work creates a special demand on your vision, and eye strain may be a particular problem that can cause or magnify headaches. Eye strain and its implications were discussed earlier, but if your glasses fit too tightly or they are not suitable for the intensive work that you do, they should be changed. Frequent vision breaks should be taken during the course of your working day.

Turning your head to one side excessively while performing your tasks or holding a telephone receiver between your neck and shoulder frequently or for long periods can also contribute to muscle fatigue, spinal instability and headaches. Pay attention to how often and for how long your head is away from a balanced and neutral position to determine if this is a possible cause for the pain you feel.

Proper posture, chair support, suitable arrangement of your work area, materials and equipment can reduce the effects which may be causing or contributing to your headaches, neck or back pain.

Previous neck or head injuries, as well as problems mentioned earlier in this chapter, can cause headaches. Fitting your work area and chair to your body and your body to your work area, as well as proper exercise and stress management techniques, can greatly reduce or eliminate headaches. If, however, your headaches persist, do not hesitate to seek professional advice.

Fatigue

Fatigue is a common complaint among workers. It is often difficult to measure, but is frequently described as a vague tiredness or feeling of low energy, lack of enthusiasm or weakness. The major causes include the things we have been talking about: poor posture and chair support, as well as not fitting into your work area or arranging your materials and equipment properly. High levels of job stress, lack of exercise and inadequate quality of sleep and rest are also to blame.

Fatigue can demoralise you and lead to the attitude: 'Who cares if I get my work done?' Your employer certainly cares about the quantity and quality of your work, and so do you, because your job depends on it. Fatigue has a subtle way of making you care less and less about your job and may even make you feel resentful at having

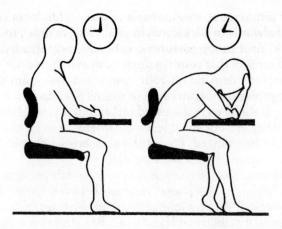

Figure 4.29 *Fatigue may show its effects as the working day passes*

to do your work. Attempting to live with fatigue is not the way to enjoy your work or feel that sense of accomplishment for a job done well, and it is no way to keep your present job nor will it lead to the possibility of promotion and economic growth for you and your family. It is difficult to go to work with the feeling that you are going to be worn out before the end of the day (Figure 4.29).

It doesn't have to be like that! One of the most common causes of physical and mental fatigue is lack of exercise. It may seem contrary, but you were given a body that was meant to move. The body is a dynamic instrument, wanting and needing exercise. Think of a camp-fire: if you add logs to the fire, it grows larger and more vigorous, and if you don't add logs, the fire burns out. If you exercise your body and give it proper nutrition, your energy is preserved, but if you don't take action to keep your fire burning, it gradually goes out. This is a rough example, but it shows you how important it is to exercise and move your body. You have a special challenge, which is different from that faced by a person who uses his or her entire body to work. You have to sit in one place to do most of your work so your body cannot get the exercise and movement it needs. These special job requirements make it necessary for you to stretch and move your body during breaks, and you should participate in either work, home or group exercise classes that will help to keep your body healthy.

You now have a better understanding of how bad work postures, as well as unsuitable or non-supportive chairs and work area arrangements, create strains in your body. These unnecessary strains can be reduced by sitting in the best possible position and adjusting your chair and work area to suit your body and your task.

5

Stress

Stress is such a prominent phenomenon in our lives today that you can hardly pick up a newspaper or magazine that doesn't have some reference to stress, its causes and effects on your body, or ways of dealing with it. In fact, mention of the word 'stress' can almost create a reaction in your body. It can be an alarming word or feeling, so let's first disarm this apparent enemy to our well-being and learn how to make it work for us instead of against us.

Understanding stress

Stress, in the simplest terms, is your physical and emotional reaction to change. It sounds almost too simple, but that's what stress is: your body's reaction to change. If you perceive the change as threatening, or you don't understand it, it can cause physical effects on your body (Figure 5.1). Your objective in this chapter is to learn how stress affects you so you can understand how to make it work for your benefit. The term 'stressor' describes the situation or circumstance which causes stress (the physical and emotional reaction).

Let's say, for instance, that you have a deadline to meet at work. You say to yourself, 'I have to get this done by four o'clock.' Your body tenses. You know you must meet the deadline, so you focus your attention and concentrate on the task in hand, and you finish the task by four o'clock. You experience a feeling of exhilaration, pat yourself on the back for a job well done and then relax for a while and let your body unwind.

The stressor involved your awareness that the task had to be

Figure 5.1 *The cumulative effects of uncontrolled stress can make you lose enthusiasm for your work*

performed within a certain time limit. Your body and mind responded by performing the task, and then you relaxed and felt good about your accomplishment and your contribution to the operation of the company or business. During this stress cycle, certain things probably happened in your body of which you may or may not have been consciously aware. Your body geared up to accommodate the stress of the job in hand. Your muscles tensed, your jaw clenched, your pulse rate increased, your blood pressure went up, your hands may have become a bit cold and clammy and your stomach may have tensed (Figure 5.2). These body reactions are quite normal; they are the physical reactions to stress.

Now suppose you regarded the stress of having to finish this particular task by four o'clock as overwhelming, and instead of considering it a challenge to be overcome, you were afraid you would not be able to meet the deadline or maybe even questioned your ability to perform the task at all.

Figure 5.2 *The physical effects of stress*

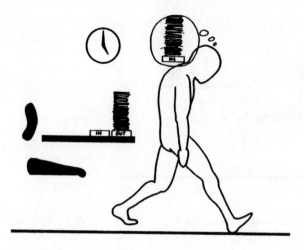

Figure 5.3 *Avoid carrying the burden of your work home*

The same reaction of muscles tensing, blood pressure rising, stomach tightening and so on would still occur, but instead of using the energy created within your body by the assignment (stressor) to focus your attention and concentrate on the task in hand, you were preoccupied with thoughts of your inability to do it properly or how hard the job is, to justify the possibility of not finishing it properly or on time. With this attitude, you will probably still be tense or stressed even if you do meet the deadline. You may worry that your employer won't approve of or will reject your work, even if it's completed properly. You may carry this heavy burden on your shoulders, and in your mind, home with you (Figure 5.3). You may not release this stress when you go to bed, so you are still tense when you try to sleep. This can result in restless sleep, and you will still be tense when you wake up. You will try to get through the next stressful day, still carrying the weight of the previous day on your shoulders. You can see that this is a vicious cycle; it is very common, and from time to time most of us get caught up in this sequence of events.

Congratulations are in order, because you have just jumped over the first hurdle in understanding and dealing with stress. That first step is to understand that it usually isn't stress or a stressor that is the problem. We all experience this type of pressure, but it's the way we perceive and handle the stress or challenge that is the key. If you perceive stress as a burden or heavy weight on your shoulders, you may question your own ability to cope, and you will get locked into its negative effects. This drains your positive attitude and self-confidence, and robs you of the enjoyment and satisfaction you should receive from performing your job well. Remember, you were hired because your employer had confidence in you and your ability to perform tasks to help make the business prosper.

On the other hand, if you see the tasks before you as a challenge to be overcome and you decide to take on that challenge and do your work using your unique abilities, you will not only increase your concentration and thus work better, but you will also feel better about yourself and experience a sense of accomplishment from having successfully performed your duties.

We all know people who seem to thrive on stress. It's as if they were saying, 'Bring on the challenge! I'm ready and I will do whatever it takes to meet it in the best way I can.' This sense of taking on challenges instead of being overcome by problems, combined with a feeling of commitment to conquer or succeed, can make the apparent stresses that lie before you seem fun. You can learn to enjoy the stresses and challenges that you face, not only in your work but also in your personal and family life, by changing your attitude and the way you see your daily challenges.

Job stress creates an energy within your body that is vented not only in physical responses but also in your concentration on your work. You need to know how to release or let go of this stress to enable you and your body to recuperate and recharge so you can meet the next day's stresses and challenges with enthusiasm and vigour. Inability to vent the energy derived from meeting stress will make the physical effects of stress accumulate within your body and mind and can cause or contribute to health disorders such as emotional conditions, digestive troubles and high blood pressure, as well as causing or intensifying headaches, neck and back pain.

Some say life is not a bed of roses, but I disagree. Life can be a bed of roses! You can experience the beauty of the rosebuds and flowers, as well as the rich green leaves surrounding the bloom, but every stem grows with sharp thorns. The beauty of the rose can overpower the pain of the thorn, or the thorn can keep you from plucking the rose. Nobody floats through life without experiencing difficulties, misfortune and sorrow, but if you concentrate only on the thorns, you will never see the beauty of the rose. It's your choice.

A healthy reaction to stress involves not only the way you perceive stress, but also the way you reverse or counteract its physical effects. The stress reaction gears you up inside, and in order

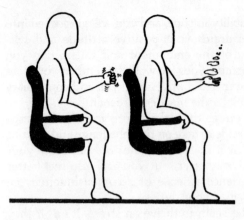

Figure 5.4 *Progressive relaxation*

to prevent this pent-up energy from accumulating in your body, you have to shift gears. This means slowing down and using relaxation or special breathing techniques, as well as engaging in some form of enjoyable physical exertion such as aerobics, swimming, cycling or tennis, to use up or give vent to the inner energy built up during periods of stress. This shifting of gears, both higher through enjoyable exercise and lower through relaxation techniques, will help to keep stress from accumulating and getting you down.

Let's look at relaxation techniques. There are many different techniques, but some of the most common and easy to follow are progressive relaxation, positive imagery, deep breathing and focusing (Figure 5.4). If you would rather set about stress reduction or one of the other techniques described in this book with the help of a qualified practitioner, be sure to do so.

Progressive relaxation

Progressive relaxation was developed by Edmund Jacobson in the early 1900s. The theory is that when we experience mental stress, we tense our muscles, and the physical discomfort of knotted muscles makes our mental stress worse. The objective is to break the tense mind–tense muscle cycle.

Progressive relaxation consists of alternately tensing and then relaxing different groups of muscles, forcing you to focus on how it feels to relax. Here are 11 simple steps to be taken:

1. Sit in a comfortable chair or lie on the floor with your feet against the wall, and close your eyes.

2. Make a tight fist with your right hand, hold it for about five seconds and experience the tension.

3. Unclench and let the tension flow out, noting how different it feels to relax.

4. Do the same with your left hand and the muscles in your upper arms and shoulders.

5. Tense your neck, hold and then relax, noting the feeling of relaxed tension.

6. Frown as hard as you can and then relax.

7. Smile as hard as you can and then relax. (Remember how it feels to smile and be sure to use these muscles more than your frowning muscles.)

8. Raise your toes (or push against the wall), feeling the leg tension, and then relax. Again, notice how the tension drains away.

9. Take a deep breath, feeling the tension in your chest. Breathe out and then relax. Breathe in again and hold, then breathe out and concentrate on how calm you are.

10. Conjure up in your mind a peaceful, pleasant setting and enjoy it for a while.

11. Now count slowly to four and open your eyes. You will be fully alert and relaxed.

A daily session using this technique may take about 20 minutes at first, but with practice it can be much shorter. The technique may be impractical to follow at work, but if you set aside the time and make a habit of using progressive relaxation daily, not only will your work and job satisfaction benefit, but also your general health and well-being.

Deep breathing

Deep breathing is another simple technique used to help combat the tension build-up experienced by most office workers. Just follow these easy steps:

1. Sit in your chair or stand comfortably, but erect.

2. Place the palms of your hands against your stomach.

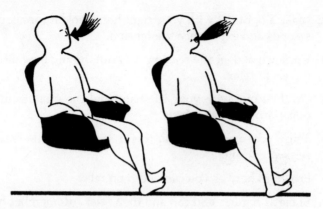

Figure 5.5 *Deep breathing*

3. Breathe in slowly through your nose, but allowing your stomach to expand forwards against your hands.

4. Hold this deep breath for a few seconds.

5. Breathe out slowly through your mouth, pursing your lips slightly, and feel the tension draining away.

6. When you have breathed out as much as you can, repeat the technique.

You should repeat this cycle a couple of times at first and work up to taking four or five breaths in this manner after some practice. Be careful not to breathe too fast as this may cause hyperventilation or lightheadedness. If this is the case, even after you have performed the technique properly, seek professional advice. This technique can also be performed in short breaks during your working day, as well as at home.

Positive imagery

Another less time-consuming but enjoyable method of relaxing your mind is through positive imagery or controlled daydreams. Follow these simple steps:

1. Lean back in your chair and get as comfortable as possible.

2. Breathe in slowly through your nose and out through your mouth about ten times with your eyes closed.

Figure 5.6 *Positive imagery*

3. As you breathe out, say to yourself, 'calm', or 'relax', or just 'mmm'.

4. After about two minutes, picture a positive, beautiful, peaceful scene from your own experience and imagine yourself in it. Stay engrossed in the scene until you feel the tension drain away from you.

5. Open your eyes, get out of your chair, stretch, and you will be ready to go.

You may be able to use this technique in mini-breaks during office hours, as well as at home.

Focusing

Focusing is another valuable method of identifying and dealing with stress. (This technique was developed by psychologist Eugene Gendlin.) This is a way of recognising your body's signals that something is wrong, that your body is reacting to stressors with tensed muscles or gritted teeth. Take a 'strain inventory' every day. Check situations that might be stressful and that keep you from feeling good. First, you need to recognise how stress affects your body, whether it is in tense neck muscles or back muscles, headaches or stomach aches. Once you know this, you can write down which stressors affect you and to what degree. If you write them down, you have a better chance of finding solutions to counteract the effects. By this focusing or analysing you can gain a sense of control over stress and find yourself in a better position to adapt to the changes you encounter.

Helpful relaxing practices

Monitoring your food and fluid intake can be helpful. Caffeine is a stimulant, and while you may feel alert for a short time after taking it, you will soon feel sluggish, anxious and irritable and you may find it more difficult to concentrate on your work. Eliminate various items from your diet and see how you feel. The consumption of meat, cheese, eggs, nuts, vegetables, fruit, fruit juices and water instead of sweets, caffeine and highly processed food may help you to meet work and life challenges in a more relaxed and positive way. Withdrawal symptoms such as headaches and fatigue can occur when you remove refined sugar and caffeine from your diet; if necessary, consult your doctor.

The concepts, philosophies and techniques of yoga can be extremely effective in overcoming the tensing effects of stress. Deep, rhythmic breathing combined with slow, controlled stretching certainly deserves careful consideration. There are many good books and classes available nowadays. If you decide to start doing yoga on your own, be sure to take proper precautions. You may need supervision or professional guidance.

The feeling of soft tissue stretching and relaxing experienced by a good massage can also help to counteract the cumulative tensing effects of stress. Massage should only be administered by properly qualified individuals. It may be wise to check with your doctor before starting a course of massage.

The techniques discussed so far have taught you how to shift to a lower gear, to relax your body and thereby counteract the effects of stress. You have also learned that you must discover your major causes of stress so that you can pay particular attention to them when organising your stress management plan. It is essential to form the habit of practising stress reduction daily not only to survive but to thrive in the pressure-filled work arena, as well as in personal and family life.

Exercise

Not let's learn how to shift to a higher gear in order to burn up and give vent to some of the effects of stress (Figure 5.7). Your body

Figure 5.7 *Shifting to a higher gear through exercise helps to give vent to the effects of stress*

produces chemicals during periods of stress which mobilise it in a 'fight or flight' response. But you are sitting in a chair and using limited movements to perform your tasks. The muscles are tensed and your body is prepared for vigorous or quick activity that seldom takes place.

Structured physical exercise can be an extremely effective method of reducing stress. You should plan a time to vent systematically this unfulfilled instinct for physical action. Researchers have discovered that people under stress who take regular exercise stay healthier than those who don't. Many businesses have recognised the value of exercise and have installed gyms and running tracks for the benefit of their employees.

Exercise provides a physical release from the effects of stress and when this is accomplished there is usually a relaxing or calming

Figure 5.8 *Enjoyable exercise can provide a diversion from daily stress*

effect. Enjoyable exercise, as well as other hobbies, can provide a diversion from the stresses of the day, as well as providing personal fulfilment (Figure 5.8). Dr Herbert A DeVries, director of physiology at the Exercise Research Laboratory, University of California, has shown that even mild rhythmic exercise, such as regular walking or cycling, can be more effective in stress control than tranquillisers, without the adverse side-effects of these drugs.

Exercise is such an essential factor in stress management and general well-being that the next chapter is devoted entirely to this topic. Use what you can, when you can, according to your own particular schedule. Be sure to choose exercise activities you find enjoyable and beneficial or you will feel forced to do them. This may not only cause you further stress, but you will find excuses to delay, postpone or stop doing them altogether. You must exercise regularly for maximum benefit. Feel good about giving your body what it needs!

Laughter can also have a tremendous therapeutic value. Laughing at jokes, at life and at yourself can serve to put your stresses into perspective. Laughter, like vigorous exercise, not only satisfies emotional or mental needs, but it also seems to create positive chemical changes in the body that promote health and well-being. It's bound to make you feel better. Norman Cousins in his book *Anatomy of an Illness* used laughter, which he described as 'internal jogging', to help cure a stressful incurable disease.

As mentioned earlier, hobbies can also provide an important diversion from stress. We live at a marvellous time in history in which we can take advantage of many pleasurable activities. Choose hobbies you enjoy and that do not add to or compound the stress on your mind or your body. Take advantage of whatever you like doing, including music, going to the cinema, dancing or any other activity which interests you, relaxes you and refurbishes your mind.

The stress-resistant person

If you want to survive and thrive in this stressful life, you will need to work to acquire the attributes and perspective of a stress-resistant person. Two stress experts, Suzanne O Kobasa and Salvatore R Maddi, have found that people who are successful in coping with stress have three characterisics not found in the less hardy.

Unlike their colleagues who see change as a threat to their security, these hardy individuals perceive change as a natural challenge to be mastered. They regard life as strenuous, yet exciting, and welcome change as an opportunity for improvement. They also have a strong sense of commitment to themselves, their families and their jobs, as well as other important values. In contrast to less hardy people who find tasks boring or meaningless, they throw themselves enthusiastically and with maximum effort and interest into what they consider important missions.

Hardy individuals exhibit a sense of optimism or control over their lives. Unlike less hardy people who see themselves as passive victims of forces beyond their control and expect the worse, hardy individuals believe they can influence events. Instead of taking a situation at face value, they try to turn a possible negative into an advantage.

In what way will it benefit you to work hard and acquire these hardy characteristics? Drs Kobasa and Maddi have shown in their research that people who view life's stresses and change with challenge, commitment and control are only half as likely to become ill as less hardy people exposed to the same stress levels. Their inner resources proved to be more important and effective anti-stress factors than genetic make-up, relaxation methods or exercise. What is especially exciting is that these hardy characteristics, while usually learned during childhood, can be developed. It's your choice: you can do it if you are willing to change your attitude and acquire the appropriate habits.

Unnecessary stress in the workplace can come from fearing job loss, having an ill-defined job description, not understanding the function and use of your office equipment (especially computer

Figure 5.9 *You can choose to stumble over problems or conquer challenges*

Figure 5.10 *Is stress chasing you?*

terminals and keyboards), or not knowing how to deal effectively with customers or clients. Take the time to ask and learn how to perform your job and understand what is expected of you. Reducing or eliminating unknowns or grey areas in your job description and performance will significantly reduce stress at work.

Unfinished business on your desk or in your home life can also be a major contributor to stress. You may be thinking and worrying subconsciously about unfinished business, and this may prevent you from releasing stress and its effects when necessary. Finish those projects which you set out to do, or make a decision to put them behind you as soon as possible and practical. Completing your office work can be as mentally exhilarating as finishing a race, if you look at it in that way.

As you can see, stress management is essential to your health as well as your job performance and satisfaction. It is impossible to explain every aspect of stress in this book. You have a basic understanding, but you may need and want more. There are many good books on the subject, and I encourage you to read and discover more. One book you may wish to investigate is *Stress Management: A Comprehensive Guide to Wellness* by Edward A Charlesworth, PhD and Ronald G Nathan, PhD.

You can do a great deal to prevent uncontrolled stress reactions which could otherwise make you ill with headaches, backache, insomnia, depression, high blood pressure, ulcers, heart disease and so on. Take the necessary steps to turn this potential enemy into a friend. If you need to, seek professional guidance.

There is no doubt that our lives are and will continue to change rapidly these days. Your ability to survive and succeed is directly related to your ability to see, understand and adapt to these changes and take care of your body along the way.

6
Exercise

Our ancestors got plenty of exercise just going about their everyday lives. They did most of their work by hand and placed great physical demands on their bodies, day after day. Their life was rigorous and they had to have strong, hardy bodies to survive. Their exercise requirements were fulfilled by their work (Figure 6.1).

When the industrial revolution came, we began to use machines to make us more productive: muscle power was no longer the key to survival. The concept of assembly-line work came during this era, as we found that it was more efficient for a worker to assemble a small part of a product many times over. Workers learned to perform a task quickly, and companies found that they could make more products and profits in this way. This is when a major problem

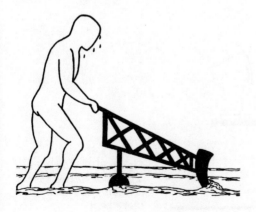

Figure 6.1 *Our ancestors exercised vigorously during their work*

developed: workers were often using only a small part of their bodies to do their work. Not only did this strain those parts that were used over and over again, but the whole body was not getting the physical exercise it needed.

Now we are on top of the wave of the information revolution. Modern advances in communications, computers and other sophisticated technology have helped to create a greater need for the production and delivery of services. Many jobs are available in manufacturing industries, but a greater number of jobs are developing in the office area. The special requirements of office and other sedentary occupations usually involve even less movement and physical exertion than work in an industrial environment.

A typical office worker has to sit for a large part of the working day with a limited ability to move (Figure 6.2). Sitting, with its special problems, combined with the tense, restrictive effects of stress and doing visually intensive work can inhibit essential, basic physical needs. Bodies were meant to move, and they react badly to this seemingly easier lifestyle. They will tend to become fat, flabby, tense and stressed, with unhealthy consequences.

Fortunately, another revolution is running parallel to the information revolution: the fitness revolution is also upon us, and it has been sorely needed (no pun intended). We are beginning to understand that the ultimate responsibility for our health is in our own hands. We make the decisions to do or not to do the things that keep us vibrant and healthy, and preserve or maintain our health. In the past, we may not have known that we could influence our health

Figure 6.2 *Sitting hour after hour causes special problems due to limited movement*

and our lives to the extent that we actually can. We now realise that we can choose either to participate and reap the benefits, or just watch and suffer the consequences. The time of the fitness revolution has come, and both participants and health professionals agree that regular exercise can produce definite benefits. Many people taking regular exercise report improved health, with fewer feelings of stress and greater job satisfaction as a result of their efforts.

Physical exercise is available in many forms and serves many purposes. We will outline how to begin an exercise programme, advising you on exercises to do before work, during your working day, and in your leisure time. We will also touch on some of the common trouble spots for people who have to sit most of the time, and give you some suggestions.

If you have a back or joint condition, heart or lung disease, high blood pressure, or have had an injury or surgery, especially if it affects your joints, muscles, ligaments or vital organs, or if you are or have been sedentary or unfit, it is recommended that you seek qualified professional guidance before starting this or any exercise programme.

First of all, let's refresh your memory. The underlying framework of your body is the skeleton. The individual bones meet each other to form joints, which are held together by ligaments. Muscles, through contraction and relaxation, move the bones at the joints. The joints are lubricated for smooth and efficient movement, and most joints have a layer of cartilage to keep the bones from rubbing against each other. The spinal vertebrae have special cushions and shock-absorbing discs between them.

Each joint is capable of a particular range of movement. The combination of all the ranges in the joints of a certain part of your body accounts for the total range of movement of that particular region. For example, your neck and head are capable of forward, backward and sideways bending, as well as rotation when all the vertebrae in the neck move at the joints.

You need to make sure that the joints move through their particular range in the proper manner to keep your body flexible. If your joints do not move adequately through their motions, the fluid lubrication cannot be replenished, the ligaments will slowly tighten and you will begin to lose movement in that joint. The spinal discs need the benefit of regular movement of the vertebrae to replenish and exchange fluids. The combination of lack of regular movement of the vertebrae and the extra pressures created by long-term sitting, especially with poor chair support or bad posture, can create fixation and instability within the joints, all of which can lead to degeneration. Fixation, misalignment and degeneration produce nerve irritation and its effects and complications include pain, muscle spasm, fatigue and organ malfunction.

Requirements of exercise

The exercise techniques you choose should fulfil several basic body needs. The first is flexibility: the exercise should move your joints safely and adequately through their normal range of movement. This concept holds true for general stretching before, during and after work, as well as warming up and cooling down from more vigorous activities, such as aerobic dancing. Next is strength development: the exercise should stretch, challenge and strengthen your muscles. You use many muscles in your daily activities, but some are used more than others. All your muscles need to be used regularly, whether at work or during exercise.

Your choice of exercise should condition your body, because you sit for a great deal of the time at work and probably do not move about vigorously. You need to choose from among the exercises that help to strengthen the heart, diaphragm and lungs. Aerobic dancing, cycling, jogging, swimming, tennis, squash, brisk walking and many other vigorous activities, when done properly, can boost and sustain

Figure 6.3 *Being a 'weekend warrior' can be hazardous for your health*

the pulse rate, making you breathe deeply and causing you to perspire. They help your body to use up oxygen more fully, improve blood cholesterol balance, lower blood pressure, aid in weight control, and help relieve stress and depression.

Finally, the exercise should promote balance and alignment. The exercise programme you follow should counteract the effects of long-term sitting and promote equal use of both sides of your body. It should counteract the tension you may feel in your shoulders, arms, neck, back or legs. Remember, one of the major ways to counteract the detrimental effects of a stressful job is to vent the energy and tension that build up within your body physically through exercise.

This does not mean you should adopt the 'weekend warrior' philosophy, going out to play a vigorous, competitive, three-hour game of tennis on a Saturday afternoon and feeling you have done enough exercise for the week (Figure 6.3). This occasional outburst of physical energy in an unconditioned body can actually be harmful and can contribute to the physical symptoms you may be experiencing during your office work. Effective exercise should be regular, consistent and enjoyable.

Now you are ready to start a programme of various exercise activities at work and during your leisure hours. You don't want to go overboard with so many hours of daily exercise that your home life suffers, but you do want to exercise effectively and efficiently enough to keep your body fit and healthy, because you know how important it is to you and your job performance. The first step is making the commitment to do the things your body needs.

You now know that the exercise you take should promote flexibility, strength, conditioning, balance and alignment. It is important for you to know where and how your body fits into each of these categories as you organise your exercise activities and routines.

Personal body inventory

Look at yourself and take a personal inventory of your body. Discover your body's present condition, and you will see what areas you need to concentrate on and where you can safely start. You may need or want professional assistance; don't risk injuring yourself at this point. Start your personal body inventory by discovering your flexibility or range of motion. Stand in front of a full-length mirror and begin with head and neck movements. Rotate your head slowly

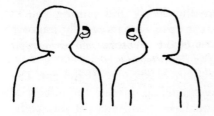

Figure 6.4 *Head rotation is usually 80 degrees to the left and to the right*

to the right and take note of where your head stops. Then turn your head to the left, noting where it stops. Look at the illustrations to see what is considered to be the 'normal motion' (Figure 6.4). Pay particular attention to whether one movement is more restricted than the opposite one. Your goal is to have normal, symmetrical movement. If one movement is much more restricted than the other, review your work and home habits carefully to see if frequent one-sided activities could be a source of the problem. Change your work area to reduce excessive one-sided movements and postures, and concentrate on stretching the restricted movements to achieve symmetrical motion. If misalignment or fixation has already occurred in the joints, you may need professional assistance to realign or free the fixation so you can proceed with your exercises safely and beneficially.

Tilt your head to the right, making sure you keep your nose straight ahead. Note this motion, then tilt to the left (Figure 6.5).

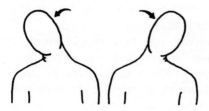

Figure 6.5 *Sideways tilting is normally 45 degrees to the left and to the right*

Look for uneven movement on either side. Bend your head down towards your chest, comparing your motion with the picture of normal movement (Figure 6.6). Repeat the process as you tilt your head slowly backwards. If any of these movements create pain or make you feel lightheaded or dizzy, seek professional assistance.

Look for painful as well as restricted motion during all movements of your neck, back, shoulders, arms, hands, legs and feet. Pain is usually an indication of trouble and you should seek medical advice before getting involved in an exercise programme.

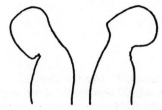

Figure 6.6 *A person can normally tilt his or her head far enough forward for the chin to touch the chest and far enough backwards to look at the ceiling directly above*

Figure 6.7 *Forward bending is usually about 90 degrees and backward bending about 30 degrees*

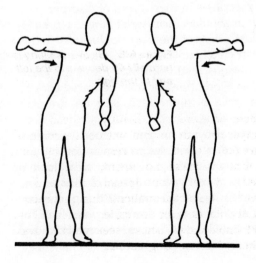

Figure 6.8 *Sideways bending is normally about 30 degrees in each direction*

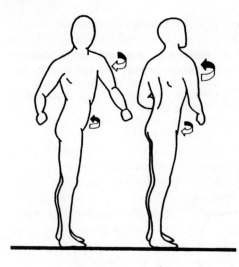

Figure 6.9 *Trunk rotation is normally 30 degrees or more in each direction*

Stand in front of the mirror and compare your body motion to the 'normal' movements illustrated in Figures 6.7, 6.8 and 6.9. It is important to mention that some people are not physically able to move their bodies through the 'normal' range of movement, even after a great deal of work. Some of this restriction could be due to unique joint formations or a previous injury or surgery, so don't strain yourself or feel a failure if you can't achieve what is considered normal motion. You are already improving yourself through your efforts. If you run into problems or have questions, ask to be referred to a doctor who specialises in these types of disorder.

You should also check your shoulder, arm, wrist, finger, leg, knee, ankle and foot motions. Illustrations of these are not included in this book, but check for unrestricted, painless, symmetrical motion in these joints. Remember, obvious restriction may mean the joints have not been exercised for a long time, or may be traced back to work or home habits, or a previous injury or surgery. Be careful of pain when stretching or exercising.

A fit body is flexible but also strong and in good condition. Muscles need to be challenged or exercised to remain strong and healthy. The characteristics of prolonged sitting with limited movement in office or sedentary work pose a special challenge. The postural muscles involved in sitting get adequate use during the day. However, if you sit badly at your desk, or don't use your chair for maximum support, these muscles will become overworked and strained. Meanwhile, other muscles are not working or challenged.

If you don't take measures to use these muscles, weakness and imbalance can occur.

Adequate and proper stretching is a very important part of exercise and fitness. An excellent book to read is *Stretching* by Bob Anderson.

Special hazards of sitting

Jan Beckwith, creator and president of Body Flex in the USA, has been a remarkable innovator in the field of low impact aerobic exercise. She has developed a 30-minute workout involving warm-up, aerobic and cool-down exercises. Many office workers follow her programme before work, during the lunch hour or after work to stretch, condition and strengthen their bodies, as well as to give vent to and counteract the stresses and strains they encounter in their work. They find it effective and enjoyable.

Mrs Beckwith has made several observations about the general physical problems sedentary workers experience. People who sit a great deal tend to develop weak abdominal, buttock and front- and inner-thigh muscles (Figure 6.10). Their neck, shoulder and back muscles tend to be tense and their spinal movements are usually restricted.

When you sit, your thighs come up towards your body and because your body is erect, the abdominal muscles relax. They relax even more if you lean over your desk to do your work. The foot, lower leg and back thigh muscles can be stretched and exercised while sitting, but the front- and inner-thigh muscles cannot be adequately stretched. As you sit, your buttock muscles bear the

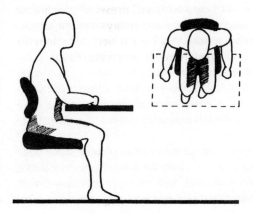

Figure 6.10 *Abdominal, buttock and front- and inner-thigh muscles are frequent trouble spots for people who sit at work*

weight of your upper body and these are difficult to stretch while sitting. You can see how problems often develop in these critical areas. You must make sure these major muscle groups get the stretching, strengthening and conditioning they need through exercise, or major structural imbalances will occur in your body and you will eventually suffer the consequences.

Your body functions as a whole, and if you use only certain parts, they may become over-strained, while the lesser-used parts become weak. Many problems can develop this way. You are now gaining the knowledge to understand the physical problems that can arise from sitting and performing your work. You can use this knowledge, and with proper work habits, postures, stress management and exercise you can neutralise or reverse the negative effects of sitting at work.

Let's learn how you can use stretching and exercising to your advantage. We will take the example of a tennis match properly played. First, you have selected good, supportive shoes, and you are wearing comfortable, non-restrictive clothing. You have a tennis racquet that is the right size and strung to accommodate your type of play, the handle chosen to fit your hand and grip. You have probably had lessons to learn how to make smooth and easy, but powerful and accurate strokes in a way that won't strain or injure you. Before the match you warm up by stretching your leg, back, neck, shoulder, arm and hand muscles and joints. You also make several practice serves and strokes in order to co-ordinate your timing.

Now you're ready to play. You concentrate and fix your attention on the ball, your opponent, his or her style of play and your own game plan. When the ball comes into your court, your body tenses a bit as you move towards it to make your shot. Between points you relax for a moment, and you stretch some of your muscles as you walk back to position. Between games you have a little more time to take a few deep breaths and stretch while thinking about your strategy. Between sets you relax and stretch a bit more as you wipe your hands and face with a towel. Then you take a few more deep breaths, and prepare yourself mentally and physically for the next set. You have learned how to stretch and relax while still concentrating on your game.

When the match is over you walk to the net and congratulate your opponent. If you are wise, you will then do a series of cool-down stretches to keep your joints flexible and let your muscles slowly unwind from the exercise and challenge you have given them. You take a warm, relaxing shower, get dressed and leave. The tennis should have been enjoyable, whether you won or lost the match; you won by giving your body vital physical exercise.

Throughout this sporting activity, though it was strenuous and demanding, you took many breaks of varying lengths to refresh your body. At the same time, you were still able to concentrate on the match. Can you imagine how hard it would be for you to stay tight and tense during the entire match? You would be worn out very quickly, and it probably wouldn't be much fun. Can you see how the same thing can happen to you at work? If you are tight and tense all day and don't take the time to stretch, relax and refresh your mind and body, you will wear yourself out. Your productivity, accuracy and consistency will suffer, and you won't get the satisfaction that you should from performing your job well. You are also more likely to suffer from some of the physical symptoms discussed earlier. There are many things you can do to control your condition.

Exercising during the working day

Let's take the concepts we discussed in the tennis match and transfer them to your office work. After all, your work can be considered a sport when a sport is broadly defined as any physical activity engaged in for pleasure and personal benefit. Your work does require physical movements, as well as the physical effort of sitting. You should obtain pleasure from overcoming the challenges and stress of your tasks, as well as a sense of accomplishment from doing your job successfully and helping in the operation of a business. Personal benefit also comes from being paid for your efforts so that you can provide for yourself and your family.

Now that we have directed our thoughts to looking at work as a sport, let's stretch, relax and exercise ourselves through the events of one day. You may be able to develop a rhythm in your work activities and stretch and exercise during breaks as described below.

The day starts when you get out of bed. You take a few moments to stretch your neck, back, arms and legs slowly before you shower, have breakfast or dress for work. If you are a morning person and an early riser, you may choose to do some type of vigorous exercise, such as jogging, swimming or aerobics after your morning stretches.

On your way to work you prepare yourself mentally for the day's tasks. You think about what needs to be done and how you are going to do it efficiently. You walk to your work area, standing erect and feeling good, and make sure that the equipment, materials, work surface and chair are arranged and adjusted to fit your body to the task. If they are not, you make the necessary changes and adjustments. You have probably been well trained in the use of your particular office equipment, so you can perform your tasks efficiently with less stress. You sit down and begin your work activities.

There are usually many occasions during the day when you can counteract some of the tension and strain that build up while you work. This can be done in much the same way as during the tennis match, when the player took breaks of varying degrees. We will call them micro-breaks, mini-breaks, macro-breaks and lunch breaks. Let's look at each of these breaks and see how you can use them effectively.

Micro-breaks

Micro-breaks are very important and can be used frequently to counteract tension build-up and fatigue in the muscles and eyes. The break may only be momentary or last up to a minute. If you have a visually demanding task, you can use a few quick and easy exercises several times an hour to reduce eye strain. You can alter your focus by looking at an object that is more than 20 feet away. Look out of the window or at a picture on a far wall. If you sit in an area divided by partitions, look up at the ceiling or lean back and look outside the partition, but make sure you don't crane your neck excessively.

Your eyes may benefit from a break from the lights in the room or your computer screen. Take a moment to place the palms of your hands lightly over your eyes while they are closed (Figure 6.11). Hold this position for 30 to 60 seconds. Avoid pressing your palms into your eyeballs. If you find that you are always looking in one direction while performing your tasks, take a moment to look in the other direction. This gives you the chance to exercise eye and neck muscles that are used less frequently.

Figure 6.11 *Take frequent vision breaks*

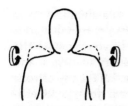

Figure 6.12 *Shrugging your shoulders in a circular movement will help the muscles to relax*

If you do a considerable amount of work with your hands on a keyboard, typewriter, calculator or telephone, you may need to exercise and stretch your fingers, hands, wrists and forearms frequently. Shrug your shoulders up towards your ears or roll them backwards and forwards in a circular movement (Figure 6.12). Turn your head slowly to one side then the other, or tilt your head slowly to one shoulder then the other.

If you are performing a stressful task, you may need a moment to take a deep breath or two. Be sure to breathe in slowly through your nose (unless you have a cold) and out through your mouth. This breathing exercise gives your body more oxygen and helps to relax the rib cage and upper body.

If you sit for long periods, find a moment to check and adjust your posture or push back into your chair's back support to stretch. You can also stretch your leg muscles by straightening your legs and moving your ankles and feet (Figure 6.13). You should have enough

Figure 6.13 *It is important to stretch less frequently used muscles during micro-breaks*

room under the work surface to move your legs about. Stray or dangling cords and wires should be attached to the wall or moved out of the way. Personal items, such as handbags, books and coats, under the work surface, should not hinder leg movement.

You won't be able to do all these exercises during each micro-break. Just use the ones that are appropriate for the type of work you do. You can alternate them, or use some and not others, according to what your body needs and responds to best. Don't fill up your working day with breaks, or interrupt the flow of your work excessively. You want to use breaks to refresh your body and improve your comfort and productivity.

Mini-breaks

Mini-breaks should occur less frequently, but will give you more time to combine a couple of different exercises or do further deep breathing, body stretches or eye exercises. Mini-breaks can be taken during a natural lull in your work activities. You have a little more time during a mini-break, so you may want to push your chair away from the work surface and bend over to stretch your back muscles (Figure 6.14), or sit and pull one knee towards your chest and hold it for five seconds before doing the same with the other leg. To be effective, this should be repeated four to six times.

An exercise known as the 'cat stretch' may be appropriate here, or during micro-breaks (Figure 6.15). Stand up at your desk and place your hands on your work surface at about shoulder width. Your feet

Figure 6.14 *Repeat this exercise five times for each leg*

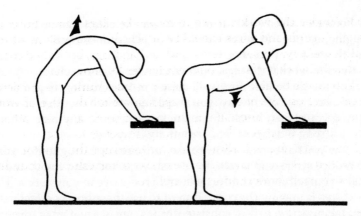

Figure 6.15 *Repeat this exercise five to ten times*

should also be about shoulder width from one another. Slowly arch your back like a cat, dropping your head towards your chest while tucking in your pelvis. Hold this position for a couple of seconds; then bend your lower back downwards while pushing your pelvis back and raising your head towards the ceiling. Hold this position for a couple of seconds. To be effective, this exercise should be repeated five to ten times. It should not be painful.

Macro-breaks

Macro-breaks are the well-known designated tea or coffee breaks. You may have 10 to 15 minutes, and you may have the chance to get out of your chair and stretch or chat with your fellow workers. You may be able to perform the cat stretch exercise during a macro-break. This may be an ideal time to divert your concentration and give your mind a break from your tasks. It's also a good time to use some of the stress reduction techniques discussed in Chapter 5. You can use positive imagery or take a stress and strain inventory of your body and do the appropriate exercises to counteract their effects.

Lunch breaks

Lunch breaks last from 30 to 60 minutes and you probably use this time to eat, do some shopping, run errands or exercise. Many large companies provide exercise facilities for their employees. If this is the case with your firm, take advantage of the provision over lunch or before or after work. If not, you may be able to go swimming, jogging, cycling, do aerobic dancing or play indoor tennis at a local health and fitness centre.

Remember that the vigorous exercise activities you choose should follow the guidelines discussed earlier in this chapter. If you sit at your desk most of the day, you should do something other than sit during your lunch break. If you are too tired to do anything but sit, it is a strong indication that something is wrong.

Now you have an idea how to use your breaks throughout the day to reduce stress and strain, to refresh your body and mind, and to make yourself more comfortable and productive in your work. The next step is making the commitment to use these breaks effectively, and taking action to do it consistently. It's simply a matter of forming the right habits.

At the end of the working day, you can do many things that you can't do in the office to help your body to unwind and to reduce the effects of stress and strain. You can practise more involved stress reduction techniques, such as progressive relaxation. You should also do an enjoyable, vigorous exercise activity that has an aerobic effect at least three to four times each week. If you are unfit or there are any special circumstances, check with your doctor before you start. You may need to work up to this level gradually. Some people find they are more inclined to exercise regularly and consistently when joining in organised workouts or sports with others.

Special exercises

There are also a few special exercises you should use to help counteract the physical effects of sitting. They involve the abdominal, buttock, front- and inner-thigh muscles, and an area in the back several inches below the shoulder blades. Study the illustrations and explanations so you can perform these exercises safely and effectively. Seek professional assistance if you have questions or there are special circumstances. Be sure to perform these exercises on a carpeted or cushioned floor.

The abdominal muscles are among the first muscles to become weak from sitting for long periods. The reverse sit-up (Figure 6.16) is a safe and effective way to exercise and begin to strengthen these muscles. Lie on your back with your arms at your sides, your palms down. Bend your knees and place your feet firmly on the floor. Raise your bent legs slowly up past the line of your breast or above your face. Then slowly return your legs and feet to the starting position.

Figure 6.16 *Repeat this exercise five to ten times*

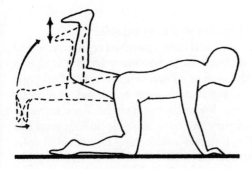

Figure 6.17 *Repeat this exercise five times for each leg*

Repeat this exercise five to ten times.

To help stretch and exercise the buttock muscles that you sit on all day, try the following exercise (Figure 6.17). Get down on your hands and knees and spread them apart to about shoulder width. Extend your left leg backwards and lift it up while keeping your back straight. Flex your foot towards your shin and bend your knee. Push your heel up towards the ceiling, using slow short lifts, always returning to hip level. Repeat this exercise five times, if it does not become uncomfortable. Repeat the entire procedure for the right side. You can repeat it more than five times for each leg if it is comfortable and not too tiring.

The thigh muscles also need help if you sit for long periods. Lie on your back with your upper body supported by your elbows (Figure 6.18). Keep your lower back pressed towards the floor. Cross your ankles and slowly raise your legs towards the ceiling while keeping your lower back and hips pressed to the floor. When your legs are vertical, slowly spread your ankles three to four feet apart without arching your back or dropping your hips. Bring your legs together and cross your ankles the opposite way. Do not bend your knees.

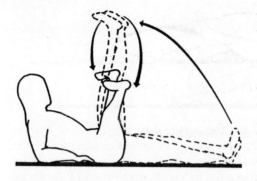

Figure 6.18 *Repeat this exercise five to ten times if comfortable*

Repeat this exercise five to ten times if comfortable.

The front thigh muscles also need to be stretched regularly. Stand with your right shoulder a couple of inches away from a wall and place your right hand on the wall or a chair (Figure 6.19). Pull your left ankle backwards and grasp it with your left hand. Roll your shoulders forward so that your lower back is straight. Bend forward slowly, using the support of the chair or wall, while pulling your left ankle upwards. You will begin to feel a stretching sensation in your left thigh. Hold at a comfortable stretching position for five seconds. Return to the upright position and repeat this procedure five times. Do the same on the opposite side.

The next exercise helps to stretch and relax that part of your back that bears a great deal of stress and strain when you lean forward in

Figure 6.19 *Stretch and hold for five seconds. Alternate legs five times each*

Figure 6.20   *Relax in this position for two to three minutes*

your chair and do not have the backrest to support you. Roll an ordinary bath towel so that it is about two inches in diameter. Sit on the floor with your legs stretched out. Place the towel under the place in your spine just above the forward curve of your lower back and several inches below your shoulder blades. Now lie down on your back with the towel in this position and relax for two to three minutes (Figure 6.20).

We have concentrated on exercising your body both during and outside work, but it is important to mention one final point. The mind and body work so closely together that it is essential for you to exercise your mind as well as your body. I will end this chapter with a quote from Dr Howard H Jan's *Success Journal*:

> Your mind, like your muscles, can either be agile or allowed to grow flabby through lack of use. Atrophy of the mind happens when you always do the same old things in the same old way, without any challenges to your mind. To exercise your mind, do something new, something different, take a walk through the woods, go to a concert, to a museum, see a thought-provoking movie, read a controversial book. Take a different route to work, eat exotic meals. Take up a new hobby or sport.

7
Sleep

Principles of sleep

During an average week you probably spend about as much time sleeping as you do working, so it is important to describe some of the characteristics of sleep and what positions are best for your body. During periods of rest and sleep your body tries to counteract the effects of the stresses and strains of your day. It recharges your battery and rejuvenates you, to help you to face what life has in store for you with enthusiasm and positive expectations. If you wake up tired and tense, it is difficult to start the day with a positive attitude.

First, let's review some facts about sleep. One of the most important facts is that it's not the quantity of sleep, but the quality of sleep you get each night that counts most. Studies by sleep

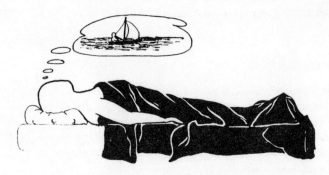

Figure 7.1 *Sleep should be an enjoyable and relaxing time*

scientists have shown that people can reduce their normal sleeping time by up to two and a half hours a night without suffering ill-effects or daytime sleepiness. If you are average, this means you are probably already getting enough sleep, but you should make every minute of this time work for the benefit of you and your body.

Sleep should be an enjoyable experience (Figure 7.1). It satisfies our deep instinctive need to feel safe and secure. We usually feel we need more sleep when we are depressed or under a great deal of stress. Sleep disorders, restless or fitful sleeping habits or poor sleeping postures can contribute to or aggravate many physical conditions such as fibrositis and degenerative arthritis, spinal instability and muscle and ligament strain. These factors may directly or indirectly contribute to back and neck aches, headaches, and other pains or symptoms you experience while performing your work. So let's consider ways of increasing the quality of your sleep and then concentrate on proper sleeping postures.

The normal sleep cycle lasts about 90 minutes; this includes the several periods of light sleep that gradually lead to very deep sleep and then back again to a light sleep. Most of us have experienced the tired, groggy feeling we get when waking during deep sleep. It's hard to get started, and we feel 'off' the entire day. It's important to try to work with our own individual sleep cycles. The following

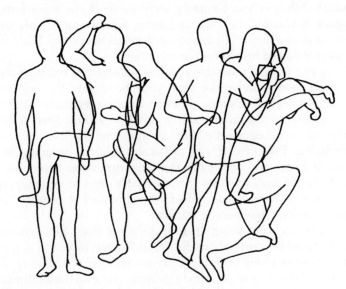

Figure 7.2 *Most people toss and turn during sleep*

111

research and clinically proved methods might help you to improve the quality of your sleep.

First, arrange for your 'sleep time' to fit in with your own sleep rhythms. A period of drowsiness brought on by a lowering of body temperature to about 97 degrees precedes sleep, whether it is ten minutes or ten hours. If you work with your natural cycle, you will probably get your best quality rest, whether it be a full night's sleep or a refreshing nap. If your drowsy period occurs at 2.30 am instead of the more usual bedtime of 11.00 pm, your quality of sleep for four hours may be more beneficial to you than eight hours of tossing and turning.

Contrary to popular desire, it may be better for you to resist the temptation for that Saturday or Sunday morning sleep-in. By getting up at the same time every morning, you reset your body clock and recycle all your sleep and waking patterns. Waking up late one day may throw out your next day's cycle. Attempt to overcome early morning drowsiness by thinking about a high-interest activity.

Sleep scientists disagree on the value of taking daytime naps. Some believe naps decrease the quantity of night-time sleep, and they are usually impractical at work. There is, however, an impressive number of 60-hour-a-week executives, as well as historic figures, who attest to the value of daytime dozing or catnaps during drowsy periods. Napoleon, Winston Churchill and Presidents Truman, Johnson and Kennedy were some of the most famous nappers. It was said of Thomas Edison, who averaged only three hours of sleep a night: 'His secret weapon was the catnap. His genius for sleep equalled his genius for invention.'

Keep to a regular timetable as far as possible. Eat balanced meals at regular times and make sure your body gets the important nutrients it needs for optimum health. Exercise regularly, but if you exercise late in the afternoon or in the evening keep it light. Exercising too vigorously late in the evening can be over-stimulating. Take care of any physical condition, including head-aches, and back and neck pains that interrupt sleep. Stress carried over from the day's activities can cause poor sleep, so you may want to practise relaxing stress-reduction techniques at bedtime. Mild body-stretching may also be relaxing.

Be cautious about using drugs to help you sleep. Sleep-inducing drugs should be used only under careful supervision and in special circumstances. Using them on your own for long periods may allow residues of the drug in your body to carry over into the daytime and cause dull thinking as well as slow reflexes. If you decide to use these drugs, be careful; they can create a dangerous cycle. You may feel drowsy and tired during the day and reach for that third, fourth or tenth cup of coffee, tea or other caffeinated beverage in order to stay awake. Then at night you will be over-stimulated by the caffeine and will reach for more sleeping pills. This artificially induced sleep-and-wakefulness cycle can have devastating effects on your body and your job performance. Don't let this happen to you. Seek professional assistance if necessary.

Alcoholic nightcaps can be almost as harmful to your health. Sleep produced by alcohol, a depressant, is of poor quality. There is little deep or dreaming sleep, and frequent awakenings are common, both from withdrawal as the body metabolises the alcohol and from the need to get up to go to the bathroom. The drug nicotine is a central nervous system stimulant, so if you smoke, stop well before bedtime. Smokers who give up the habit completely often experience dramatic improvements in the quality of their sleep.

Skip that middle-of-the-evening cup of caffeinated coffee, tea or cola, too. The stimulating effects of the caffeine in these drinks last at least six hours. Chocolate and many common pain relievers also contain caffeine and may affect the quality and quantity of your sleep.

The environment you sleep in is also important. Make it as quiet, dark and comfortable as possible. You may find it better to sleep in a slightly cool, but not cold, room. A room temperature in the mid 60s may be best, but make sure that there are no draughts or fans blowing on your body. Your mattress should be large and firm enough for comfort. Some people prefer waterbeds instead of conventional bedding as their choice of sleep support. This decision should be made by you with the help of a trusted and knowledgeable health-care professional who has a thorough understanding of your body's mechanics.

Relax before you go to bed; don't go to bed with the day's problems on your mind. The primary purpose of sleep is to relax

Figure 7.3 *Reading in bed can strain your back and neck*

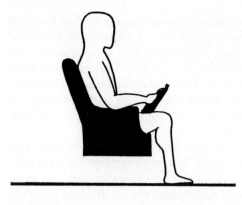

Figure 7.4 *Sit in a chair to read if you have difficulty falling asleep*

your body and prepare you for the next day's activities, so don't carry stress into your sleep – it will only cumulate within you. A good night's sleep will allow you to start fresh each day. Set aside an hour before bedtime to wind down, do something you enjoy, such as reading (adopt the proper posture), watching TV, listening to or playing music, or working on an enjoyable hobby (as long as it doesn't cause you stress or body strain).

If you like, and it doesn't interfere with your diet, have a light snack before bedtime. Research shows that people are sleepier after a high-carbohydrate snack than after one containing high protein. Try a glass of milk or other non-caffeine, non-alcoholic drink, a dish of breakfast cereal or a light sandwich. It's best to avoid peanuts, beans, most raw fruits and vegetables, as they can cause flatulence. High-fat or deep-fried snacks such as crisps should also be avoided, as they can keep your digestive system overactive.

Your inner clock will be reminded of sleep if you follow a regular routine each night before retiring. A ritual such as brushing your teeth, washing your face, setting the alarm and turning off the lights may help to signal your body to sleep. Try to follow your ritual even when you are away from home. Don't go to bed if you aren't sleepy. If you still have problems on your mind, try reading a boring or difficult book until you become sleepy. If your muscles feel as if they are tied up in knots, relax them with the techniques described in Chapter 5 on stress.

Relax in bed by stretching your body and getting comfortable. Enjoy the feeling of relaxation and warmth. Pleasant imagery can also help: imagine yourself in a relaxing scene. Let your thoughts float and don't concentrate too much on any one subject, especially on forcing yourself to fall asleep. Think about the good and pleasant

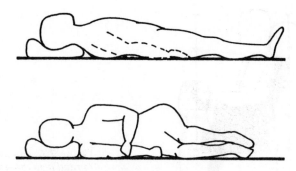

Figure 7.5 *Proper sleeping positions*

things that are happening in your life, as long as they do not make you feel too excited. If you aren't asleep in 20 minutes or so, don't just lie there worrying and fighting it. Get out of bed and go into another room. Continue your relaxing activities until you are sleepy. Wait for your drowsy period before going to bed again.

Proper sleeping positions

Now you know how important the quality of your sleep is and several ways to help you maximise its effects, but it is also important that you understand and use proper sleeping positions. You may toss and turn in your sleep, in much the way you move about while sitting in your chair at work. It's normal to move and shift in your chair, even if your body has proper support and you have good posture. Likewise, it's normal to toss and turn while sleeping, but you should have a good, supportive mattress and pillow, and you should use proper sleeping positions.

When you are sitting upright, the forces of gravity push down on the bones and discs of your spine, and your muscles and ligaments are working to support you (Figure 7.6). During sleep, you are horizontal and gravity is no longer compressing the length of your body (Figure 7.7). You need relief from the effects of gravity to maintain a healthy body, so the bedding you choose must support the weight of your body without sagging, and yet be pliable enough to accommodate the contours of your spine, hips, shoulders, neck and head. A sagging mattress or inadequately filled waterbed places extra strain on your body when you are supposed to be relaxed and supported. This prevents your body from eliminating or reducing the strains and pressures it goes through during the day, and you

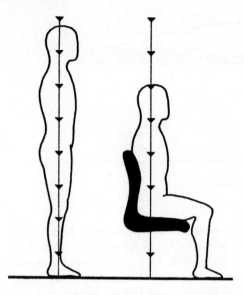

Figure 7.6 *Gravity constantly affects your body when standing and sitting*

will end up carrying strain and pressure into the next day's activities. The cumulative effect of this carrying over can aggravate many of the problems you experience during your work and other daily activities.

In previous chapters we described the negative effects that too much twisting or turning in one direction can have on your spinal, muscular and ligament balance, and how it can cause instability and nerve irritation. The same holds true for sleeping positions. If you

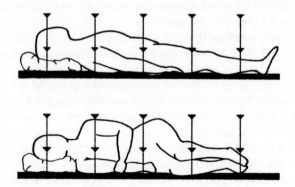

Figure 7.7 *Proper sleeping positions reduce gravity's effects on your body*

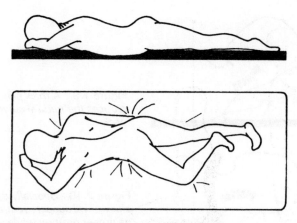

Figure 7.8 *Stomach sleeping exaggerates the curve of your lower back and forces you to sleep with your neck twisted*

sleep on your stomach most of the time, the curve of your lower back is strained (Figure 7.8); in order to breathe you have to twist your neck to one side. So here you are, sleeping or resting to reduce the effects of gravity and give your body a well-deserved break, but your spine is twisted, creating more strain.

Sleeping on your stomach or in any other strained sleeping position is particularly significant, because your body is supposed to relax. During sleep the muscles and ligaments are not standing by to hold and protect the spine as much as when you are awake. You are therefore more vulnerable to excessive ligament and muscle strain from the contortions you put your body through during sleep. In addition, your body may not recognise that it is in a twisted position, and you may stay in that position for a longer period than if you were awake. I mentioned earlier in Chapter 4 that muscle and ligament sprain and strain and spinal instability can be caused by high forces on a joint over a short period or by low forces over a long period. It's the slow, excessive or abnormal stretching through the course of your sleep, night after night, that can cause undesirable changes in your body, its balance and alignment, just as poor work posture causes strain during the day. You can effectively reduce or eliminate these problems during sleep by using properly supportive bedding and adopting better sleeping positions.

The two best sleeping positions are on your back or side. If you are already a back sleeper, then you may not have much to worry about. Be sure, however, that you use your pillow properly. Remember

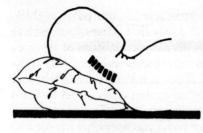

Figure 7.9 *A thick pillow reduces the natural curve of your neck*

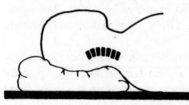

Figure 7.10 *Specially designed pillows will support your neck in its proper position while you sleep on your back*

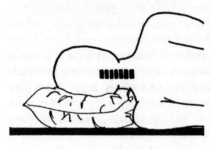

Figure 7.11 *Your pillow should fill the space between your neck and the bed to keep your neck horizontal*

Figure 7.12 *This pillow is too thin*

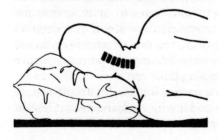

Figure 7.13 *This pillow is too thick*

that your neck should have a forward curve. If your pillow is thick, your head may rest on the pillow in a way that causes your neck to be slightly flexed (Figure 7.9). This position straightens or reverses the curve of your neck and pulls on the muscles and ligaments in the back of your neck and upper back. If you combine this with the fact that your head may be frequently or continuously tilted forward during your working day and with the tensing effect of stress on these muscles, it's easy to understand why you may have muscle and ligament strain, spinal misalignment or nerve irritation that cause neck and back pain and headaches. These problems also contribute to fatigue.

It is usually best to sleep on a flattish pillow and curl it slightly under your neck so that it supports your forward curve. Specially designed pillows that are contoured to support your neck and head properly are available (Figure 7.10), and they are well worth the modest investment. It is very important to support your spine's natural curves during sleep. Seek professional guidance when selecting one of these special pillows.

Another major consideration for back sleepers is that it is not a good idea to sleep for long periods with your arms above your head. This can put strain on your shoulders and upper arms as well as crowd the neck vertebrae and the muscles, ligaments, blood vessels and nerves between your neck and shoulders, and can cause numbness and tingling in your arms and hands.

Many of us are side sleepers, and that is also a recommended position, but there are a few tricks to proper side sleeping. Again, the pillow plays an important role: your pillow should fill the space between your neck and the bed so that your neck is level with the bed (Figure 7.11). If the pillow is too thin, your head and neck will bend towards the bed and there will be crowding and jamming of the vertebrae on the side of your neck that is closest to the bed (Figure 7.12). The shoulder on the same side may also be jammed; meanwhile, the other side of your neck is stretched. If you sleep like this night after night, imbalance and misalignment, strain and nerve irritation can occur, all of which contributes to or magnifies the strains you encounter in your work and daily life. If you sleep on your side and your pillow is too thick, the side of your neck closest to the bed is stretched and the other side may be jammed (Figure 7.13). Here too, a specially designed pillow can come to the rescue because it will support your neck so that it is level with the bed.

Avoid sleeping with your arm under your neck and head. This can cause a problem similar to sleeping on your back with your arms

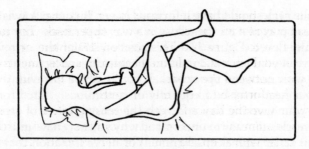

Figure 7.14 *Sleeping with your top leg in front of your lower leg causes your pelvis to rotate and your spine to twist*

above your head. Try to tuck your shoulder slightly forward with your forearm across your stomach or resting on the bed.

When you sleep on your side, your legs should be on top of each other with your knees bent. It's very easy to throw the top leg over towards the bed, but this makes your hips twist and your pelvis and lower spine rotate (Figure 7.14). This strain, night after night, can

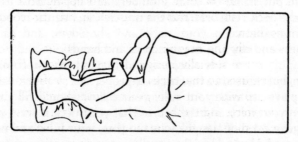

Figure 7.15 *Place your knees directly on top of each other when sleeping on your side*

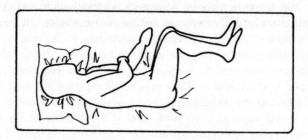

Figure 7.16 *You may place the top knee slightly behind the other*

cause the same type of strain in your lower back that a twisted or poorly supported neck can cause in your upper back. Try to keep your knees on top of each other (Figure 7.15) or the upper knee slightly behind (Figure 7.16). In many cases, it is acceptable to place a thin pillow between the knees, especially if you have bony knees and it's uncomfortable to keep them together.

Now you have the basics for good sleeping habits and positions; you have the ammunition to combat some of the problems that you may encounter with sleep and rest. All you have to do is to form the right habits. If you have problems changing some of your undesirable habits, study and apply the rules outlined for you in Chapter 8.

Caution

If you have had a neck or back condition or injury, you may be advised to sleep on your back with pillows under your knees and with your head, neck and upper back supported by several pillows. You may even be advised to sleep partially on your stomach with several pillows to support you. These are special circumstances and the advice should be followed, but after your injury has healed these positions should not become your regular sleeping postures. Consult your doctor to determine if and when you can change to a different position.

Follow carefully the manufacturer's instructions and directions for sleeping on a specially designed cervical pillow. If you have trouble getting used to that type of pillow, seek professional advice. Inability to sleep with your body properly supported and positioned may be a warning sign that you have imbalance, instability or abnormal movements in the joints of your spine which may need to be corrected. Don't allow any questions to go unanswered.

People with heart or lung disease, high blood pressure and other conditions may not be able to sleep without special support. It is not within the scope of this book to explain these particular circumstances. Therefore, if there are special circumstances, follow your doctor's advice.

8
Replacing Undesirable Habits

We are creatures of habit and, over time, we tend to become the creatures of our own particular habits. If we form the habit of slumping (Figure 8.1) or assuming awkward postures (Figure 8.2) at our desks, exercising very little and allowing the effects of stress to accumulate in our bodies without forming the habits required to counteract these strains, our bodies will become unbalanced, inflexible, tight, irritated and fatigued. We will be more likely to suffer physical degeneration and ill health as well as missing the enjoyment we should experience in our lives both at work and at home.

Habits are usually learned responses acquired over a period of

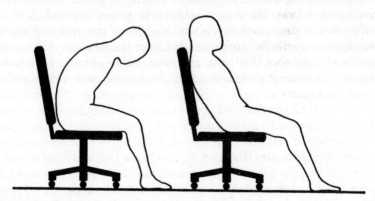

Figure 8.1 *Slumping can be hazardous to your health*

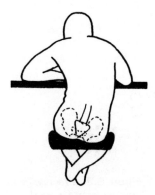

Figure 8.2 *Assuming unbalanced postures creates strain on your body*

time. They begin in the conscious mind and are assimilated into the subconscious. After a habit has been learned by the subconscious, it becomes automatic, or second nature, because you don't have to think consciously about what you are doing. The routines we go through day after day are filled with major and minor patterns. Our days are largely programmed by habits. If you stop and think for a moment, it's amazing the extent to which our daily lives are built around our habits. If many of these habits are undesirable or bad for you, their effects will appear over a period of time. You may unintentionally have programmed the wrong responses into your subconscious mind. This causes you to respond in the way you have conditioned yourself to feel and act, no matter how negative, false, distorted or destructive it might be. Consequently, you must go through a period of unlearning or deprogramming in order to replace bad habits with good ones.

After reading this book, you have a better understanding of how your body works, the way in which the unique circumstances of office work can adversely affect you, and the many possible solutions to particular problems. You have learned how your work area and chair should fit you, and how you need to fit your body properly to your office surroundings. You know how factors in the work environment such as lighting, temperature, draughts and noise can affect you, your job performance and enjoyment, as well as ways of dealing with them. You have learned how to sit properly for your particular task and how to ease or counteract the stresses and strains you encounter (Figure 8.3). You know that you need to 'shift gears' during the day to escape the cumulative effects of stress on your body – shifting down a gear through relaxation techniques (Figure 8.4), and up through enjoyable physical exercise (Figure 8.5)

123

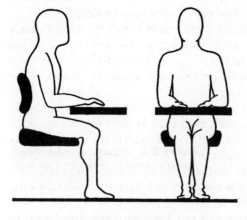

Figure 8.3 *Practise good posture habits at work and at home*

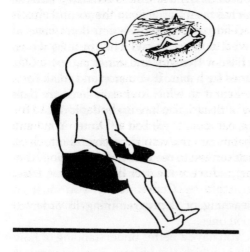

Figure 8.4 *Shift to a lower gear to relax from the effects of stress*

Figure 8.5 *Shift to a higher gear to vent stress physically*

to vent the pent-up energies within your body created by stress and the sedentary nature of your work. You have come to understand that your body must be flexible, well balanced and aligned or it may lose some of its capabilities and you will suffer problems and pain. You have read many of the common symptoms that sedentary workers experience, some of their causes and you know how to improve or correct them. You even know how to sleep better.

It seems to be an awful lot to remember, but it's all extremely important to you and your well-being, as well as your job performance and satisfaction. You should keep this book handy for reference and always seek professional guidance if you have persistent problems or questions.

Many of the bad habits you have formed unintentionally should now be apparent to you, and it is to your benefit to take action to replace them with good habits. This requires effort, but if you follow steps outlined in the remainder of this chapter, you can do it. Don't be discouraged if you have many habits to change. Most of us do! The most important thing is simply to get started. It will take time and effort, but the rewards will be well worth it.

No amount of will power is of any use unless we really want to give up old habits. We generally want to give up the painful effects of our habits, but are not willing to give up the habits themselves. If you feel you are being forced to replace a bad habit by a good one, you will start feeling deprived or that you are sacrificing too much. This creates negative feelings such as guilt, frustration and anxiety, as well as stress, which make it impossible to change for more than a short time. It's a matter of attitude. You have to be dedicated to the idea and motivated by the benefits it will bring. Do not condemn yourself for having bad habits or condemn the habits themselves. Getting angry with yourself can also cause the negative feelings that produce resistance to change. Accept the fact that you have a bad habit you want to replace with a good habit.

Make a list of the habits you want to change. This will allow you

Figure 8.6 *Changing undesirable habits is a challenge, not a problem*

to keep track of them and enable you to check your progress. It is a personal list and you do not have to show it to anyone unless you want to. Then jot down how you are going to change those habits, or which desirable habits you are going to replace them by. Write down the easiest and most logical way of accomplishing this. Visualise yourself as having already succeeded in changing your habits. See yourself enjoying the benefits of your new positive habits. Pat yourself on the back for taking the necessary action to accomplish your goals. Observe your actions and note every time you fail to do what you promised yourself. Remember, do not condemn or scold yourself. Simply make an objective observation and allow yourself to make the necessary correction. Keep a record for at least 21 days. You are actually using conscious thought and action to retrain your subconscious mind so the new habits will become automatic, or second nature. You can train your conscious and subconscious thoughts, just as you can train or exercise your body physically to get in shape. It may be difficult at first, but it gets easier as you stick to your programme.

You can promise yourself anything, but bear in mind that the important thing is to make the commitment to replace the bad habits with good ones. Don't put it off. Start now! Once you are successful in changing a habit, you will not only gain the benefits of the more desirable habit, but you will also begin to gain in self-confidence, by knowing that you are improving yourself. You may even build up some of that enthusiasm for work and enjoying life that has dwindled over the years.

The Choice
Is Yours!

Knowledge, action and consistency are the keys which unlock the doors for a brighter, healthier future for you. You can learn not only to survive but thrive in your chosen occupation. You have been provided with much of the knowledge you need to understand your body and your work area, as well as methods for taking action to improve yourself and your surroundings. It is up to you to use this knowledge and act accordingly to enhance the quality of your life and your work. It is essential that you are consistent in your efforts. Without consistent action you will fall back into the old ways of doing things.

Health and happiness are a journey and not a destination. Consistent positive action will make your journey through life more pleasant and fulfilling. Do you want merely to exist and survive, or thrive and enjoy? It's your choice.

Appendix

The quality of your life is in your hands! In order to determine what measures you should take to improve your level of positive well-being, you must have an idea of the suitability of your current lifestyle. Circle the appropriate answers to the questions in the four sections of the Personal Lifestyle Inventory. The section on p. 130 will tell you how to mark your answers and interpret the results. (The Personal Lifestyle Inventory was organised and developed by Thomas M Wolff, APR, editor of *Staying Well*, a bi-monthly newsletter published by the Foundation for Chiropractic Education and Research.)

1. Personal Lifestyle Inventory

(Circle answer A, B or C for each question)

General
1. How do you rate your own health and vitality compared with that of others your age and sex?
   A Extremely healthy, very energetic. **B** Average health and energy. **C** In poor health, tired a lot.

2. Do you smoke?
   A No. **B** Smoke less than 10 cigarettes or 5 cigars a day. **C** Smoke more than 10 cigarettes or 5 cigars.

3. Do you drink alochol?
   A Up to 7 drinks a week. **B** 8 to 15 drinks a week. **C** More than 15 drinks a week. (A drink is a shot of spirits, half a pint of beer or a glass of wine.)

4. Do you wear a seatbelt in the back seat of a car?
   A Always. **B** Sometimes. **C** Never.

5. Do you seek professional advice from your doctor or other health specialist when you have symptoms or conditions that need attention?
   A Always. **B** Sometimes. **C** Never.

   Sub-total_____

Stress

6. Do tension and worries interfere with your daily activities or relationships or contribute to headaches or pain in the neck, shoulders or back?
   A Seldom. **B** Occasionally. **C** Frequently.

7. Do you use tranquillisers or alcohol in an attempt to relieve tension?
   A Never. **B** Sometimes. **C** Frequently.

8. Do you find time each day to relax your mind and your body?
   A Yes. **B** Sometimes. **C** Never.

9. How many hours of restful sleep do you get each night?
   A 6 to 8 hours. **B** More than 9 hours. **C** Less than 5 hours.

10. Do you cope with stress by such methods as setting realistic goals, building close relationships, leisure activities, humour and exercise?
    A Yes, generally. **B** Some of these. **C** No.

    Sub-total_____

Nutrition

11. Are you overweight or underweight?
    A No. **B** By 5 to 19 lb. **C** By 20 or more lb.

12. Does your daily diet include something from each of the four basic food groups: (1) meat, fish, poultry, eggs, nuts; (2) milk and milk products; (3) whole-grain bread and cereals; (4) fruit and vegetables?
    A Every day. **B** Three times a week. **C** Seldom.

13. Do you limit your fat and salt intake? Which of these does your diet most resemble?
A Vegetables, fruit, lean meat only, no extra salt. **B** Meat, eggs, cheese 12 to 24 times a week, little salt. **C** Meat, cheese, eggs, whole milk, snacks more than 24 times a week, lots of salt.

14. Do you limit sugar and have enough fibre intake? Pick the diet nearest your own.
A Whole-grain cereals, fruit and vegetables, practically no sugar. **B** Mixed whole-grain and white bread, fruit and vegetables, little sugar. **C** Heavy on desserts, sugar, white bread, low on vegetables and desserts.

15. Does your breakfast contain a third of your daily requirement for calories, proteins and vitamins?
A Frequently. **B** Three times a week. **C** Seldom or never.

Sub-total_____

Exercise

16. How much physical effort do you expend on your job and other physical activities (such as housework, mowing the lawn, etc)?
A A great deal. **B** Moderate amount. **C** Very little.

17. Do you participate in vigorous physical exercise?
A At least half an hour, three times a week. **B** Once a week. **C** Occasionally or never. ('Vigorous exercise' will cause you to perspire and raise your pulse rate to over 120.)

18. How far do you walk briskly, jog or run per day?
A More than a mile. **B** Less than a mile. **C** Virtually not at all.

19. Do you climb up and down stairs instead of taking the lift and walk instead of drive, when feasible?
A Usually. **B** Occasionally. **C** Never.

20. Do you stretch and bend a few minutes each day to keep your body flexible?
A Usually. **B** Occasionally. **C** Never.

Sub-total_____
Grand total_____

Marking and interpretation
Give yourself five points for each A answer, three points for each B answer and one point for each C answer. Mark each of the four sections and add the points together to get a grand total.

If you have a total score of 90 to 100, you rate Excellent. You have a strong awareness of sensible lifestyle habits in all areas and you practise them.

If you have a total score of 75 to 89, your ranking is Good. You are above average in sensible habits and with minimum improvements, you could be excellent.

If you have a total score of 61 to 74 your ranking is Poor. You have a number of lifestyle habits that are potential health problems.

If you have a total score of below 60, you are in a risk area. With effort, you can modify your habits and overcome potential health hazards.

2. Nutrition

There are many theories and philosophies concerning nutrition. This section gives you an outline of the basic concepts involved in a balanced diet. Certain health conditions may require special nutritional considerations so do not hesitate to seek professional assistance.

Sedentary workers differ from their counterparts doing heavy manual work not only in their tasks, but also their nutritional requirements. Occupations involving much physical exertion may require workers to consume 3000 to 5000 calories per day. People who earn their living sitting in an office use less physical energy, so their calorie expenditure may only be 2000 to 3000 calories per day. Consequently, sedentary workers should be more concerned about the quality than the quantity of their food intake. It is advisable to cut down on energy-rich and highly refined or processed foods in favour of more natural foods such as vegetables, fruit, whole-grain bread, natural dairy products and lean meat.

With this in mind, let's review some basic concepts about nutrition. In the last few years, the medical profession and other health advisory bodies have suggested that a healthy diet should be based on the following guidelines:

1. Eat a variety of foods.
2. Keep to a desirable weight.
3. Avoid too much fat, saturated fat and cholesterol.
4. Eat foods containing adequate starch and fibre.
5. Avoid too much sugar.
6. Avoid too much salt.
7. If you drink alcohol, do so in moderation.

The foods and liquids you eat, digest and assimilate build and maintain all the cells of your body and provide the energy you need to live and work. If you do not give your body the proper nutrients and fuel for energy, you cannot have and maintain good health. You should therefore strive for a balanced diet that includes the four basic food groups (fruit and vegetables; bread, grains and cereals; protein; and dairy products) plus one other essential element, water.

Fruit and vegetables provide healthy complex carbohydrates for energy, plus fibre and minerals, as well as Vitamins A, B and C. At least four servings a day from this group are recommended.

Whole-grain or enriched bread, cooked or dry cereal, pasta, rice, oats and corn also provide healthy complex carbohydrates plus Vitamin B, protein, iron and fibre. Four servings a day from this group are also recommended.

Lean meat, poultry, fish, eggs, pulses, nuts, seeds, peanut butter and soya products provide protein, essential amino-acids, fat, iron, fibre and Vitamins A, B and E. Two servings a day are recommended.

Dairy products provide calcium, amino-acids, and are often enriched to provide Vitamin D. Adult men require two servings a day but adult women and children who need extra calcium should have four servings a day. Low-fat dairy products are usually preferable.

An essential element of a balanced diet that is often neglected is water. Water not only refreshes the fluids of our bodies, but it is also essential in many of the chemical reactions that are required for life. Under normal circumstances our bodies need two and a half fluid ounces of water for each two pounds of body weight every day. For instance, if you weigh 9 stone 2lb you should drink one gallon of water a day. Coffee, tea and other beverages are not an adequate substitute for fresh water. Do not take this concept to extremes and drink large quantities of other fluids such as coffee, tea, soft drinks etc in addition to the amount of water you should be drinking. Certain health conditions such as high blood pressure and kidney, heart or lung problems may require limited fluid intake. If necessary, consult your doctor before you increase your water consumption.

The best source of nutrition comes from natural, unprocessed foods, but we live in an era in which highly-processed and preserved foods are so easy to obtain that they readily become a major source of our food intake. For this reason, nutritional supplements may be useful. There are many nutritional supplements available in health food shops and chemists, but it is always advisable to consult your doctor before taking a course of extra vitamins, minerals etc as they can sometimes do more harm than good.

3. The orthopaedic or kneeling chair

One of the most frequent questions I am asked when speaking to groups of office workers about chairs concerns the orthopaedic or kneeling chair. As you can see from the illustration, the kneeling chair represents an intriguing new concept in chair design. One of the major theories is that when the thighs slope downwards to this degree, the curve of the lower back assumes its natural position more easily. I have sat in several of these chairs and personally find them very comfortable. I have not, however, used this chair for extended periods of time, nor have I discovered any research into the effects of this type of chair on the long-term, high-frequency user.

Areas of possible concern are: the effect on the circulation in the legs and feet; the effect of prolonged knee pressure from the kneeling pads; the effect on the ankles and feet of the positions in which they are maintained; the adjustability of the chair to fit a wide range of work areas and tasks. (For example, can you safely and comfortably bend, twist and reach in the various positions your tasks require while using this type of chair?) Another area of concern is the chair's capacity to allow the user to assume the three common sitting postures discussed in Chapter 2 (work-intensive, conversational and relaxation). The use of this type of chair may require a higher work surface in order to keep you from slumping forward. This would present a problem if your work area was not adjustable. If a person using this type of chair begins to experience leg, knee, ankle, foot or other symptoms, he or she should obtain a different chair and consult a qualified health professional.

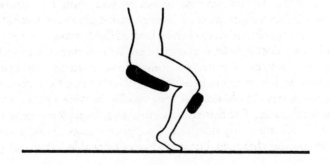

Clearly, this type of seating has its advantages in helping people sit more comfortably and correctly. I have seen patients with significant back problems become more comfortable and productive from its use. Whether it fits you and your tasks is something that requires careful consideration and evaluation. It will be interesting to watch its use and popularity in the future.

Bibliography

The following titles have all been published in the United Kingdom.

Anderson, B, *Stretching*. Pelham Books, London, 1981.

Cetron, M, and O'Toole, T, *Encounters with the Future: A Forecast of Life into the 21st Century*. McGraw-Hill, Maidenhead, 1983.

Charlesworth, E A, and Nathan, R G, *Stress Management: A Comprehensive Guide to Wellness*. Corgi, London, 1987.

Grandjean, E, *Ergonomics of the Home*. Taylor & Francis, London, 1973.

Grandjean, E, *Fitting the Task to the Man: An Ergonomic Approach*. Taylor & Francis, London, 1980.

Hoppenfield, S, *Physical Examination of the Spine and Extremities*. Appleton-Century-Crofts, New York, 1976.

Leach, R A, and Phillips, R B, *Chiropractic Theories: A Synopsis of Scientific Research*. Williams & Wilkins, Baltimore, US, 1985.

Lueder, R K, *The Ergonomics Payoff: A Guide to Designing the Electronic Office*. Holt, Rinehart & Winston, Toronto, 1986.

Maltz, M, *Psycho-Cybernetics*. Pocket Books, New York (nd): Wilshire, Los Angeles, 1967.

Naisbitt, J, *Megatrends: Ten New Directions Transforming Our Lives*. Futura, London, 1984.

Naisbitt, J, and Aburdene, P, *Reinventing the Corporation: Transforming Your Job and Your Company for the New Information Society*. Futura, London, 1986.

Selye, H, *Stress Without Distress*. Corgi, London, 1987.

Ziglar, Z, *See You at the Top*. Pelican, Gretna, US; Insight Editions, Worthing, 1985.

To the Reader

Dear Reader,

I am very interested in helping you to grow through better health and in your chosen occupation. It is important that I know how you feel about the information presented in *Fit for Work* and how the book might be enhanced to help you and others even more.

Your comments will be most helpful as I evaluate the book for future editions. Please answer the following questions and return this form to me at Parallel Integration, PO Box 6001, Lincoln, NE 68506, USA. I appreciate your time and help.

Sincerely,

Scott W Donkin, DC

1. What is your occupation? _____

2. What did you like most about this book? _____

_____

_____

3. What did you like least about this book? _____

_____

_____

4. Which sections helped you the most? _____

_____

_____

5. Which section helped you the least? _____

_____

_____

6. What additional information would make *Fit For Work*
more helpful? _____

_____

_____

_____

7. Other comments and suggestions: _____

_____

_____

☐ Please send other related information.

Those of you involved in policy decisions for companies, businesses and government agencies are faced with the difficult task of meeting the challenges of today's business environment. You are already aware of the important role your human resources play in reaching your business goals. Parallel Integration can help you to create and maintain a healthier and more productive atmosphere for your human resources.

For more information, please write to:

Parallel Integration
PO Box 6001
Lincoln, Nebraska 68506